# MY JOURNEY

*"An Inspiring and Intriguing Autobiography that deals with Overcoming Adversity and Achieving Against the Odds"*

Lincoln Butler Sr.

# My Journey

Copyright Page

**Published by Lincoln Butler Sr.**

**Year of Publication 2023**

Copyright © 2023 Lincoln Butler Sr.

All rights reserved. This book or any portion thereof may not be reproduced or used in any manner whatsoever without expressed written permission of the publisher except for the use of brief quotations in a book review or scholarly journal.

# My Journey

*"Where one begins does not have to determine where one ends up. Your origins and background do not limit your potential."* Dr. Israel Tribble

# Dedication

This book is dedicated to my wife, three sons, and grandchildren. I leave this autobiography as part of my legacy to each of you. Hopefully, after reading *My Journey*, you will have gained a better understanding of who I am, how I became who I am, and why I made some of my life decisions. I love and respect each of you more than I can describe, and I pray that I have lived my life honorably enough to have earned your love and respect. Also, I pray that each of you, **and other readers**, will benefit greatly from this story and be challenged and inspired to become all that God has designed you to be.

This book is also dedicated to the memory of my dear mother, Cathryn Naomi Butler, my father, Charlie James Butler, and my brothers: Robert, Larry, and Lawrence Wilbur Butler.

# My Journey

I now welcome and encourage each of you to join me as we explore *MY JOURNEY*!

## MY FAMILY

**The Butlers**
Front Row (L to R): Dishon, DiJuan, Dirrick, Jr.
Middle Row (L to R): Lincoln Sr., Dorothy, Duncan, Jillian
Back Row (L to R): Teneisha, Lincoln Jr., Sherry, Dirrick Sr., Justin, Michael

Dirrick L. Butler II, Grandson

# My Journey

## **Acknowledgments**

I am grateful to my wife for being my "best friend" and the love of my life! No one succeeds without support and encouragement from others. You have been there **'For Me and With Me'** from *our* very beginning.

The path that I chose in life took us across the country, which meant that we had to pack up everything we owned, relocate to other states *(Arkansas, Michigan, New York, and Texas)*, and then try to get re-established all over again each time we moved. In some marriages, this could easily have been the beginning of the end.

But you never complained, nor did you ever try to discourage me. Instead, you always *encouraged* me to follow my dreams, and then you were there by my side to help me achieve those dreams in every possible way that you could.

Also, I thank you for helping me recall some specific details about various aspects of our life together. So, this story about *my journey* is also about *your journey* because, without YOU, there would be no ME! I love you, and I thank God for you!

To my "Two Big Brothers and life-long friends," Robert (Bobby) Butler, Sr. and Acy L. Butler, Sr., thank you guys for

# My Journey

**never** treating me like a *"little brother,"* WELL, EXCEPT FOR THE TIME WHEN THE TWO OF YOU TRIED TO *S-T-R-E-T-C-H* me because you thought that I was too short!

Other than that time, you guys have always made me feel like I belonged and that there was nothing that I couldn't do. Bobby, thank you for trusting me enough to keep your 1956 Red and White Chevy Bel Air down on the college campus while you were completing some of your army training. It really made me feel special riding around on campus with my sweetheart *(Snow)* in that awesome car! I love you guys and have always taken pride in calling the two of you **"My Big Brothers!"**

Thanks to my "Golfing Buddies," William and Bobby, for being my biggest competitors on the golf course. Man, we had some really "crazy" times out there, challenging each other to be the best golfers we could be. The Bible says *Iron sharpens Iron*. We truly did help each other become better golfers through the many heated discussions *(arguments)* we would have while competing.

I will forever cherish the memories. William, thanks also for being such a "solid decision-maker" and always "keeping it real!" I have gained much from our discussions

# My Journey

about *handling our business* and personal obligations in our home life.

Acy, thank you for being "my memory" while writing this book and for helping me to recall many things I had either forgotten or, in some cases, never knew. It is amazing how *you* remember our past with such clarity. It's like you have "total recall."

You have always told me how much you love me. In fact, I just received a message from you a few days ago, and it simply read, **"Linc, the word BROTHER does not do justice to the way I feel about you. I LOVE YOU, MY BROTHER."** Acy, I am grateful for your love and friendship, and yes, I love you too, BIG BRO.

I am also deeply indebted to each of my other siblings *(Larry, Brenda, Stanley, Linda, and Kathy)* for always making me believe I can do anything that I set my mind to. Thank you for your unconditional love, encouragement, and support. It means the world to me. I love you guys more than you will ever know.

To my dear friend and brother, Thurman Gilbert, thank you for your love, encouragement, and support that reaches all the way back to our freshmen year in college (1965). We have always been there for each other, and I thank you for taking this journey with

# My Journey

me. My story would not be complete without sharing some of our experiences as brothers!

Many thanks to my good friend and colleague, Dr. Elmore Toomer, for encouraging me for years to write this autobiography. Toomer, you kept saying to me, *"Lincoln, you have a story to tell, and if you don't tell it, it will never be told."* Thank you, my friend, for providing the "push" I needed to make this happen.

Thanks to my good friend, fraternity brother, and college classmate, Brother Bernard Snowden. You are always so positive and uplifting. Your belief in my abilities and constant encouragement helps to keep me motivated and inspired to help others. Thank you, my friend.

To Elsie Moffitt, thank you for nudging me to write my memoir. Instead, I decided to write an *autobiography* to tell my whole story. Thanks for the encouragement.

I am also extremely grateful to the thousands of teachers, students, parents, colleagues, and supervisors I had the privilege of knowing and working with during my career. I learned so much from each of you, and I will forever treasure the memories.

# My Journey

## Foreword by: Dr. John L. Mack

When you read *"My Journey,"* it feels as if it's *Your Journey.* Every riveting and revealing page removes another layer of Lincoln Butler's life. The names could have been anyone's but when you read it, you can feel comfortable putting your name in the blanks. I loved every minute as I leaned in and looked at a slice of his soul.

It felt weirdly eerie, as if he had witnessed my life and lived it out as his own. I can see the audience resonating with everything. Lincoln Butler has lived a life of Significance and Excellence.

# My Journey

This Amazing Journey could have been anyone's story, from meeting his Snow Queen on the first day of college to rising in the ranks of the Educational Community. Then achieving the goal of Principal, and recognition by his peers for the African American Educators Hall of Fame Induction. Finally, raising a family and becoming a conscious citizen committed to Excellence and Integrity. As he transitioned from location to location to ultimately settling in Dallas, Texas, he discovered himself along the way and helped countless others find their way.

Lincoln Butler's story is everyone's journey to finding themselves despite racism or any other actual or imagined reasons that try to trip people up and prevent them from reaching the pinnacle of their success. Lincoln pours equal amounts of power and pain onto every page as he shares the passion, purpose, and principles needed to succeed. His parents did their best to prepare him for a society that did not welcome him with open arms

**"My Journey"** is a Truly Great American story complete with all the ugliness, uniqueness, and awesomeness that makes America Great.

Lincoln tells this story with no hidden agenda or no adverse aspirations. You're going to laugh when he talks

## My Journey

about UFOs. You'll cry when he talks about the debilitating disease that made him walk away from the very thing he loved. All in between, he weaves a tapestry of intrigue, influence, and impact.

Prepare to be entertained and educated (I call it **Entertainucation)** as you experience all the makings of a movie that will make you Laugh, Cry and Aspire to be your very best. Yes, this is ***My Journey*** too. And when you read it, it will become yours as well.

Dr. John L. Mack ~ *"The Self-Publishing Strategist"*

# My Journey

## Table of Contents

| | |
|---|---|
| Dedication | 3 |
| **Acknowledgments** | 5 |
| Foreword by: Dr. John L. Mack | 9 |
| Introduction | 13 |
| Chapter I: The Beginning | 17 |
| Chapter II: My Hometown - Brinkley, Arkansas | 33 |
| Chapter III: My Parents | 39 |
| **Chapter IV: Content from Mama's 1989 Scrapbook** | 77 |
| **Chapter V: Grandparents, Special Uncles and Aunts** | 103 |
| Chapter VI: Attending Public School | 117 |
| Chapter VII: Off To College | 159 |
| Chapter VIII: Living and Teaching In Brinkley, AR | 187 |
| Chapter IX: Life in Flint, Michigan | 193 |
| Chapter X: Life in "The Big Apple" | 197 |
| Chapter XI: Dallas, Texas | 221 |
| Chapter XII: The Principalship & Other Admin Assignments | 241 |
| Chapter XIII: Community/Volunteer Service | 321 |
| Chapter XIV: It's Q & A Time | 329 |
| Chapter XV: Summary – Three Phases of Our Life Together | 335 |
| **APPENDICES** | 339 |
| **Appendix A:** | 339 |
| Words of Encouragement | 352 |

# My Journey

## Introduction

Growing up in a rural and very segregated little southern town certainly had its disadvantages, but there were also some advantages. For example, our student body was "all black," and all our teachers were also black. I am proud to say most of those teachers cared about us and held us to pretty high standards. They nurtured us and did everything they could to prepare us for life and the **REAL** world that awaited us.

After I enrolled in college, my favorite elementary teacher, Mrs. Bennie Bryant, asked me what foreign language I was planning to take. Well, most of my homeboys who were ahead of me in college were either taking or had already taken French. They made it sound so cool: *Parlez-vous Francais*? This enticed me to take French as well. So, I told Mrs. Bryant I was going to take French. She immediately asked me if I was going to live in France

# My Journey

because she said that was about the only place I would get to use it. She strongly suggested I take Spanish. She reminded me that Mexico bordered the United States and the Spanish-speaking population would continue to migrate to this country and enter the schools. She said we would have to communicate with the students and the parents, so it made a lot more sense to take Spanish.

Well, for once, I did not listen to Mrs. Bryant's suggestions and have *regretted it to this day*. I strongly believe I would have significantly benefited from many more opportunities if I had become fluent in Spanish. *Lesson Learned: Listen to your teachers, not your homeboys!*

On another note, as I think back over the years, I can remember a lot of things my sons and I did together. I particularly enjoyed our time on the basketball court at my school, W. W. Bushman, playing ball against my brothers, cousins, and friends. That's where I believe my sons developed some of their "toughness." Also, as I think back, I don't remember my sons asking me questions about *my life* and how things were when I was growing up. So, hopefully, as this autobiography is read, the answers to questions like those listed below and many more will be revealed:

1. What was my life like during my childhood and teenage years?

# My Journey

2. How did I meet my wife?
3. When did I know that I was in love with my wife?
4. Why did we get married at age 19?
5. What were my parents and grandparents like?
6. Why didn't I join the army like my brothers?
7. How and when did I lose most of the vision in my left eye?
8. Why did we move so often *(from state to state)* when we were young?
9. Why did I start lifting weights?
10. Why do I refer to Thurman Gilbert as my brother?
11. Why was I principal at T. W. Browne Middle School for only one year?
12. Why did I initially retire so young? *(I was 54 when I first retired in June 2002.)*

# My Journey

# My Journey

## Chapter I: The Beginning

*"Peter! Peter! Get your a\*\* in here. You little Puny Bastard!"*

As a young boy, I can still hear my father calling for me. You see, my father had "Special Names" for the first five of his children he sometimes used when referring to us if he was angry or upset about something. Oddly enough, he referred to *some of us* so often in this manner one would have thought our last name was *Bastard. (Well, maybe that's exaggerating a bit.)*

Hi, I am Lincoln Butler, Sr., and *this* is **My Journey**. My father named me after my mother's oldest sister's husband, "Abraham **Lincoln** Fox." My mother objected to my father adding

## My Journey

"Abraham" to my name, so they settled on just naming me Lincoln. Mama said daddy had a deep admiration and respect for Uncle Lincoln and therefore wanted me to have his name. I don't recall ever meeting Uncle Lincoln Fox.

**Lincoln Butler, Sr.**     **Uncle Abraham Lincoln Fox**
(Aunt Amanda's Husband)

I was born September 12, 1947, in Toledo, Ohio, at 120 Roff
Street, now a residential, *vacant* lot in Toledo, Ohio. I don't know the exact reason my parents left Brinkley, Arkansas, and moved to Toledo, but I do know my father's oldest brother, Andrew, was already living there. So, I am guessing he encouraged them to move there for better economic opportunities.

In 2007, my wife and I went to Flint, Michigan, for a family reunion. While planning for this trip, I decided to arrive a day early so we could go to Toledo, Ohio, to find my birthplace. Over the years, this had become something I felt the need to do, and Toledo

# My Journey

is only 108 miles from Flint. *(You know, it's amazing how some things become more important to you as you age. You see, I lived in Flint, Michigan, for two years, and prior to that, I spent the first two summers out of high school in Flint. During those times, it was never a burning desire for me to drive to Toledo to check out my birthplace.)*

But anyway, back to 2007. After arriving in Toledo, we had no problem finding where I was born because the address is on my birth certificate. To our surprise, it is now a *vacant lot*. Nonetheless, it was truly an exhilarating feeling for me to be standing on the grounds where I first came into existence. I was 59 years old, and this was the first time I had stepped foot on that soil since we lived there back in the late forties. This was indeed an awesome and humbling experience for me. My mind conjured up thoughts about what life may have been like for my parents and what they did for a living. Where did they shop? Did they attend church? What did they do for entertainment? I am sure my mother did not have much of a social life because she already had two young children *(Bobby was about 3½ years old, and Acy was almost two)* when I came along.

As mentioned earlier, my father's brother, Andrew, had been living in Toledo for a few years. My brother, Acy, said

# My Journey

Andrew was a factory worker. Sadly, Andrew died from a heart attack at the young age of 48. I attended his funeral in Fargo, Arkansas.

While I was there at the location of my birth, I did some videotaping and took photos of the vacant lot and the surrounding area. Below is one of the pictures I took of the empty lot. This is where I opened my eyes for the first time! Praise God!

**Location Where I Was Born**

After residing in Toledo, Ohio, for a while, my mother left my father and moved to Chicago, Illinois, where we lived with family members for a short time. My mother said she left Toledo because, in her own words, *"I was running away from your daddy."*

# My Journey

When I asked mama why she was running away from daddy, she said they were not getting along well and she *"ran away all the time."* Mama said my father showed up looking for her in Chicago sometime later. She said they talked and eventually worked out their differences. Subsequently, she eventually moved us back to Toledo.

After a year or so back in Toledo, daddy and mama packed us up and moved back to Brinkley, Arkansas. I am not sure why they left Toledo. These events took place between 1947-1949.

Immediately after returning to Brinkley, our family moved into the home where *"The Banks Family"* lived. However, we eventually settled into what would become "our family home" down the street in a house given to my mother by her parents.

**OUR FAMILY HOME**

# My Journey

**This is the home I grew up in; I also got married in this house. (This was just my preference!)**

*NOTE: Our home did not always look like this because during the early '60s, my parents had some renovations and remodeling done to upgrade it with modern "in-door" plumbing, running water, gas heating, a modern kitchen, etc.*

Prior to the renovations, we got our water from a pump in the backyard. Our heating came from a "wood-burning" stove, and we used fans in the summer to help cool the house. In the winter, my two older brothers (Bobby and Acy) and I would "take turns" getting up each morning and starting a fire in the stove so the house would warm before everyone else got up. The house would be extremely cold before the fire started burning. After the renovations, our home contained three small bedrooms, one bathroom, a den, a kitchen, and a living room. The upgraded appliances included gas stoves for heating the house, an electric stove for cooking, and a/c window units for cooling. We also continued using oscillating fans.

Our home was the last house on the left side of the road on a dead-end street in a section of town known as the "West End." Our address was 409 W. Union St., Brinkley, Arkansas. Playfully, I often tease my wife about living in the projects in Tuscaloosa,

# My Journey

Alabama. I call her *"My little project girl!"* She immediately comes back with *"At least our project was brand new, and we were one of the first families to move in. So, I lived in a beautiful new brick home while you lived on the West End on a* **DEAD-END STREET***!"* We often have a good laugh when we start talking about this and how we grew up.

At some point later, the city did connect our street with the street behind our home, so it was no longer a dead-end street. My extended family members *(uncles, aunts, cousins, and maternal grandparents)* also lived in this neighborhood on the West End.

One interesting thing I remember about the street we lived on was dirt *and lots of mud when it rained.* Eventually, the city covered the road with rocks, which certainly was a good thing. However, there was just one little problem with this project. The city stopped pouring the rocks about 30-40 yards before reaching our home. I remember hearing the "grown folks" saying someone on that end of the street *had not paid their taxes.*

Therefore, it affected the other homeowners, like us, who had paid their taxes. Bottom line, when it rained, my brothers and I still had to navigate the mud until we reached the section of the road where the rocks began. Strangely enough, with all that mud on the road, my father would still raise "*holy hell*" if he came home from work and found mud on our shoes.

## FEARLESS OR INSANE

**ROCK FIGHTS**

As I think back over some of the things we did as kids, I often wonder if we were FEARLESS or just plain INSANE! I remember one of the "crazy" games we *(brothers and cousins)* used to play on the road in front of our home. We would have what we called "rock fights." This was where two groups of us would face off a short distance away from each other. Members of both groups would assemble piles of rocks before the game began. Then the members in both groups would start hurling rocks at the opposing group at full force.

This was extremely dangerous. Some of those flat rocks, frequently had a way of *curving back in on you* and finding their mark! As I look back on this, I tremble at what could have happened to some of us while playing such a dangerous game, e.g., eye injuries, busted lips, teeth knocked out, head injuries, etc. But thankfully, I don't remember anyone being seriously hurt.

# My Journey

**Some of the brothers & cousins (Butlers, Marshalls & Smiths) who engaged in the rock fights.**

As a result of the constant ducking and dodging while throwing the rocks, some of us became very good athletes. Perhaps this may have improved our agility, footwork, and overall athleticism. My cousin, David Smith, Jr., *a.k.a. Hook*, was an exceptional athlete and outstanding in every sport he played. He could also "handle his business" if anyone wanted to start a fight with him! My brother Bobby was a very good overall athlete and a tremendous boxer and golfer. Fred Marshall was an outstanding

# My Journey

football player. Rodger was a very good golfer. I was "pretty good" in basketball but nowhere near as good as Hook, who was more than a year younger than me. We both played guards on the same basketball team. I also became a pretty good golfer over the years!

**ALACAZAM**

Another adventure that stands out in my mind during my adolescence is when we built a "tree house" deep out into the woods. We called it "Alacazam!" We got this name from a TV show we had seen. We drafted our rules for governing ourselves and swore to secrecy we would not tell outsiders about our tree house. Whenever we wanted to go hang out at Alacazam and other kids were with us, someone in *our group* would simply say, "Alacazam!" All the members of our group would begin to discreetly disperse, making excuses like they had to go home or something. After we got away from the "outsiders," we would run as fast as we could and eventually dash into the woods. Once we got to our tree house, we would settle down and talk about different things that young adolescent boys discuss. I am certain *girls* were usually at the top of the list. Having the tree house really made us all feel special.

## My Journey

Like I said earlier, Alacazam was located deep into the woods, and one day we were exploring the area and came upon this ditch. My cousin, Rodger Marshall, and I decided to jump over the ditch as we explored the surroundings. As soon as I landed along the edge of the ditch, Rodger was landing right next to me. HOLY CRAP! As we looked down, there was this HUGE SNAKE just inches from where we had landed. It was probably a poisonous water moccasin. I was so scared I don't even remember turning around to make the jump back across the ditch. I honestly think I jumped back across the ditch backward! My adrenaline was pumping so fast, and I was hysterical. Rodger was in just as bad a shape. Why that BIG snake did not bite one of us still boggles my mind, yet I am grateful and thankful we escaped without being harmed. It's amazing how, as kids, we never really thought about the dangers lurking around a ditch deep into the woods surrounded by weeds nearly as tall as us.

However, usually in every group, there seems to be a BOLD one. That day, luckily, there were two bold ones with us, my brother Acy and Rodger's brother, Fred Marshall. Both were about 1½ years older than me. They gave new meaning to the word bold and certainly were not afraid of snakes. So, Rodger and I nervously showed them where we had encountered the snake, and

## My Journey

they both jumped to the other side and began thrashing around in the weeds until they found the snake!

Looking back, I know that snake did not deserve to die. It was not bothering anyone and was minding its own business out in the wilderness. But my brother and cousin, fearless as they were, commenced beating that snake until they killed it. We then brought it back to the tree house to examine it. I remember we decided to stretch the snake out across the entrance of our tree house to "scare people away" if they wandered upon our house. As kids, I guess we never thought the snake would decompose right there in front of our tree house. Well, it did, and we had to remove its remains.

A few weeks later, we got together and went out to Alacazam to hang out like we frequently did, and to our dismay, someone had found our tree house and demolished it. We were crushed! It felt like someone had violated us! Why would they do this? We weren't bothering anyone. We were just a small group of brothers and cousins who enjoyed hanging out and talking about life and what we wanted to do when we became adults. I remember we often discussed buying a big house so all of us could live together. I guess that's how kids think.

In the meantime, we never knew who destroyed our home, but we always believed some hunters came upon it and decided to tear it down. Or, it may have been the "landowners" who found it and destroyed it to keep us off their property. We never built another tree house in the woods.

**SWIMMING IN A MUD-HOLE**

My cousins, Fred and Rodger Marshall lived in Wichita and Salina, Kansas, during some of their childhood and adolescent years. They became very good swimmers. After they moved back to Brinkley, there was no swimming pool for Blacks to swim in. So, we found a large ditch *(a mud hole),* and Fred and Rodger started trying to teach us how to swim. I don't know how much we learned, but we had a great time. Then one day, a White dude, probably in his late twenties, came upon us and demanded that we "get the hell out of there" and go home. We were too young to rebel against him, so we got out of the water. But Fred, who never liked being disrespected or treated unfairly, angrily dived back into the water and began swimming again.

The White guy became very agitated when Fred would not get back out of the water, so he waded into the water and physically pulled Fred out. We were all extremely upset because we weren't doing anything wrong or bothering anyone. We were just having fun together while trying to learn how to swim. I don't know if that

## My Journey

was his property or not. But that was just how "White folks" in the South treated Black people in those days because they knew they could get away with it. Looking back now, I am sure we could have easily taken that guy, but in those days, it was not wise for Blacks to get into altercations with White people.

The bottom line is if Blacks wanted to get along and stay out of trouble, they had to *"stay in their place!"* Plus, if we had gotten into an altercation with him, our parents would have probably whipped us for being out there swimming in a mud hole and for fighting with a White adult. Anyway, we left and went home. *You know, I don't think we ever thought about the fact that there were probably snakes in and around that ditch too.*

### FINALLY, A REAL SWIMMING POOL

At some point during my high school days, we began traveling to Forest City, a neighboring town about 25 miles east of Brinkley. One of the fathers, Mr. Buster Webster, owned a truck and started loading us up on Sundays and driving us to Forest City to swim in a "real swimming pool." He charged us twenty-five cents each for the round trip. Because of our excitement and anticipation of swimming, it seemed like it always took forever to get there.

# My Journey

I remember the first time we arrived at the swimming pool. It was beautiful! Like all the other kids, I was so hyped and ready to jump into the pool, only to be stopped by the pool attendant who instructed us to rinse off under the shower before getting in the pool. This was new to us, but we had a GREAT time once we got into the pool. It was truly exhilarating and exciting! Every Sunday thereafter, we looked forward to swimming *in a real swimming pool*.

Some of us managed to save enough money to buy some "frog fins" and started swimming with them whenever we went to Forest City. Amazingly, once you take the fins off, you realize you cannot swim nearly as well as you thought with the fins on.

So, my advice to all beginning swimmers is learn to swim without this type of swimming gear because, in my opinion, it hinders your progress as a new swimmer. Going to Forest City on Sundays to swim was certainly one of the joys and highlights of my adolescent years.

# My Journey

# My Journey

## Chapter II: My Hometown - Brinkley, Arkansas

When I grew up in Brinkley, it was a small, segregated, rural town where Blacks and Whites attended separate schools and did not mix in any way. The population during that time was around four thousand.

*"Hate is too great a burden to bear. It injures the hater more than it injures the hated."*

**Coretta Scott King**

## SEGREGATION AND RACISM

### MOVIE THEATER

Negroes *(or Colored* as we were called) were required to sit in the balcony of the theater. We entered the theater through a door from the alley. Once inside the door, there was a *very small*

# My Journey

*space* with two little windows. The window on the left was where we paid for our theater ticket, and the one on the right was the concession stand. After leaving the concession window, we would climb the dimly lit stairs to the balcony and find our seats.

Conversely, the White people entered the theater from the main street into a very spacious and attractive lobby and then strolled to the theater to take their seats.

**DRINKING FOUNTAINS**

Whites had refrigerated drinking fountains on the inside of business establishments labeled WHITES. Blacks drank from antiquated, usually "unrefrigerated," water fountains located outside of business establishments *(around the side of the building)* with a sign above the fountain that read **COLORED!**

**DOCTOR'S OFFICES**

The doctors' offices had separate entrances and waiting rooms for Blacks and Whites.

**SCHOOL TEXTBOOKS**

Most of the textbooks we used were outdated books sent to our school from the White school. They would use the books for several years, and when the district purchased a new edition, they would send us the old texts. When we got the books, many times there would be no spaces available to write our names because the White students had used them for several years prior.

**PUBLIC LIBRARY**

Blacks were NOT allowed to use the public library in Brinkley even though Black parents paid taxes too. I remember one of my friends, who was a couple of grades ahead of me, was home on a break from college and went to the library to conduct some research. He shared that he was denied entry and was told that "Coloreds" were not permitted to be in the library. This was in 1965!

**SWIMMING POOL**

Shortly after I moved away from Brinkley in 1970, the city built a swimming pool but would NOT allow Blacks to swim in it, even though Blacks paid city taxes just like the Whites did. I understand the Black people protested and raised so much hell until the city officials eventually had the pool *filled in with dirt and closed it down* just to keep Blacks out!

**GOLF COURSE**

# My Journey

Brinkley has had a golf course since 1903, but Blacks were NOT allowed on the course because it was "FOR WHITES ONLY!" As recent as 2017, my brother, William, was in Brinkley and drove out to the course to see if he could play a round. He was immediately told, "NO!" William asked if it was a public course and was told it was *"sort of private"* and the only way he could play on the course was to be invited by someone.

Well, we all know that meant he would need an invitation from a White person to play the course. First, he didn't know any White people in Brinkley; and secondly, even if he did, what White person would invite him out to the course? This was 2017, and this degree of "racism" still existed in Brinkley.

This is probably the main reason the population is so low in Brinkley. Most people move away from this type of blatant racism when they graduate from high school or college.

### CHOPPING AND PICKING COTTON

Our school system operated on what was known as a "split session." This was done so Black people could "chop" and "pick" the White man's cotton. The chopping season was around June and July.

# My Journey

Now, let me clarify something here. Although it was called "chopping cotton" we really didn't chop the cotton. We chopped the weeds from around the little cotton stalks because if not removed, the weeds would choke out the cotton, causing the crop to be of little profit for the owners.

We would chop cotton most of the summer in the blazing hot sun. When you got thirsty, there was a "water boy" *(or sometimes maybe a water girl)* who would go up and down the rows serving water from a large, galvanized bucket with an aluminum dipper. Everyone drank from the same dipper.

Even as a youngster, I had a BIG problem with this because I would see some of the older folks spit out their snuff and tobacco, and often you would see it on their lips and dripping from their mouths. I thought this was SO Gross! Also, each time someone took a drink, the dipper would be placed back in the bucket of water to give the next person a drink. Ugh! Disgusting.

As I said, I had a huge problem with this, but when you work in temperatures of 90 degrees and above, you must rehydrate yourself or pass out from a heat stroke. By the way, we didn't have *bottled water* back in those days, so we had NO choice but to drink that filthy water. There was also someone called a "straw boss," who oversaw the field and made sure everyone maintained a steady

## My Journey

gait and did not fall behind the group. The straw boss also kept the hoes sharpened.

After chopping cotton for the entire day, I would receive half of what the adults made. If they received $2.50 per day, then I received $1.25 for chopping in that dirt all day long in the blazing hot sun! I was told the reason I was only paid half the money the adults got was because I was so young and had to have help from others to keep up.

We also got blisters from holding the "hoes" in our hands all day. Because I was not making much money working in the cotton fields, my parents started keeping me home to "babysit" my younger siblings. I was elated and glad to be taken out of the cotton fields. Hallelujah!

By the way, my brothers and I also had to spend time on our grandfather's farm in the summer and fall, chopping and picking his cotton for free.

# My Journey

## Chapter III: My Parents

*"We never know the love of a parent till we become parents ourselves."* Henry Ward Beecher

**Mr. & Mrs. Charlie James and Cathryn Naomi Butler**

**DADDY**

My father's name is **Charlie James Butler.** He was born June 24, 1924, in Louisiana to Andrew and Curlie Butler. He died on October 12, 1992, in Chicago, Illinois, at the age of 68. The cause of death was a heart

## My Journey

attack. He had been ill for several years because of a stroke he suffered when he was only 58 years old.

Charlie James Butler

### MEMORIES I HAVE OF MY FATHER

Growing up at home, the four older guys called our father "**My Daddy**." For example, if we needed to say something to him, we would not just say, "Daddy, will you...." Instead, we would say, "My daddy, will you...." I couldn't remember how we started calling him "my daddy," so I asked Acy about it. For some reason, Acy has a wonderful memory and can recall many things from the past that I have either forgotten or never knew. Anyway, Acy said big mama *(daddy's mother)* is the one who started this.

Daddy would sometimes take us out to Fargo when he visited his parents. While there, big mama would play with us,

# My Journey

point to daddy, and say, "That's my daddy; that's my daddy!" Because of this constant repetition of "my daddy," we just naturally started saying "my daddy" when referring to daddy. It was not until after college that I could look my father in the eyes and simply call him *daddy*. Acy said he could never break the habit and called him "my daddy" until he died.

Daddy called me "Peter" because when I was born, one of my mother's sisters (Aunt Dorothy) nicknamed me "Pee Wee" and daddy didn't like it. So, he started calling me Peter. I still don't understand why Aunt Dorothy called me Pee Wee. It's not like I was a tiny baby. Heck, I weighed 7.0 lbs. at birth.

My father was very strict. He would get very upset with us if he came home and found paper, litter or trash in the yard. *(I guess that's why I get upset if I see even a cigarette butt on my property.)* Another thing *(quirk)* I remember about my father was as we were getting ready for school and he was getting ready for work, he would tell us if we wanted to catch a ride "uptown" with him, we had better be in the car when he got ready to leave. And folks, I mean IN THE CAR! As Acy and I recently laughed about this, we recalled even if we were reaching for the handle of the car door, daddy would drive off without us. When he said, *"Be in the car,"* that is exactly what he meant: Be **IN** the car!

# My Journey

As a very young child, I also recall seeing my father, grandfather, and some other men, pounding long pipes deep into the ground in the backyard to find water. They would then install a **hand pump.** This is how we got our water for drinking and all other uses for a few years.

I remember how we had to "prime the pump" before the water would come out, and we would catch it in a bucket. As I think about that now, I wonder, "How did they know where to drill the pipes and how did they know when they had drilled deep enough to reach sufficient water to come through the pipes?" *(Well, since I first pondered these questions, I have researched and watched some videos on this topic and found it very interesting.)*

**BEST EDUCATIONAL ADVICE FROM MY FATHER**

My father encouraged me to *read and study beyond my homework assignments* to stay ahead and not get behind. I also remember once, when my father was sick, he called me over to the chair where he was sitting and said, *"Peter, when I die, I want you to have my watch."* Wow, as a naïve, eight or nine-year-old youngster, I was honored and felt very special!

# My Journey

Man, my father would give me his watch when he died. That was probably around 1955 or 1956. The problem was, my father didn't die until 1992, so I never got that watch! And, as a child, I was not internalizing that my father would have to actually *die* for this to happen. I was just thinking about getting that watch.

My parents had ten children; one child, Lawrence Wilbur, only lived a day and a half. His navel cord was not tied properly by the "midwife," and he bled to death while in bed with my mother. A neighbor had stopped by our home to see how mama and the baby were doing.

Mama told her they were doing fine, and then she pulled back the covers to show off her baby boy, only to see all the blood drained from his little body. He was dead. I remember my mother and father were devastated. We were all standing around sad, not knowing what to do. I remember my father placing him in a shoebox and they buried him in Fargo.

**MY FATHER WAS VERY TALENTED**

He sang in a gospel quartet called "The Brinkley Harmonizers." They sang in some churches in and around the Brinkley area and surrounding towns. They also sang on the radio some Sunday mornings before church. In addition to singing, he was an "outdoorsman." He was good at hunting *(many types of wildlife)* and fishing. He was also good at playing checkers and was very mechanically inclined. I used to say if it could be broken, he could probably fix it! I remember he repaired his cars, radios, televisions, washing machines, etc. He could also fix most electrical and plumbing problems and do some carpentry work. I remember he laid the hardwood floor in our home. He could also calculate numbers in his head quickly. After I left home, my younger brother, William, told me daddy also learned to hit golf balls quite well. He said daddy only had three golf balls and would hit them out in an open field next to our home, and then William would have to go and retrieve them, only to keep repeating the process.

**SMOKING IN FRONT OF MY FATHER**

My father was employed as a deliveryman for Dixie Furniture Company for all my years growing up at home and after I went to college. I remember the first time I smoked a cigarette in front of him. We were riding in the company truck after making a delivery when suddenly I got this strong urge to light up a cigarette. I sat there, extremely nervous, debating whether to take that risk, not knowing what my father might do. YOU HAVE TO HAVE

## My Journey

KNOWN MY FATHER TO APPRECIATE WHY I HAD SUCH RESERVATIONS ABOUT LIGHTING UP THAT CIGARETTE. I had never smoked in front of him; in fact, he had no idea I smoked. As I said earlier, he was very strict! But something was burning inside me to take this opportunity to assert my autonomy and establish myself before him as a man. I was seventeen, and at that moment, I was not sure if I would live to see eighteen once I lit that cigarette. But the urge to light up became stronger and stronger until I couldn't take it anymore. So, I reached inside my shirt, retrieved my pack of Winston Cigarettes and nervously pulled one out.

I stared straight ahead *(hey, there was no way I was going to allow myself to look in his direction)* thinking at any given moment, he would aggressively snatch that cigarette from my hand and follow up with some very choice words leaving me "shaking in my boots." But, *hmm, so far, so good.*

I then reached into my pocket, grabbed my lighter, and "fired that bad boy up." I remember taking that first *LONG* drag off that Winston thinking this may turn out to be the biggest mistake I had ever made in my short life! To my surprise, there was TOTAL SILENCE. He didn't say a word. MY FATHER DID NOT UTTER A SINGLE WORD! As we continued traveling down the

## My Journey

road in the company truck, I felt a sense of freedom and relief. My God, I did it! I had stood my ground and mustered up the courage to take the first step toward establishing myself as a man in my father's eyes.

This was not done in defiance of my father; instead, it was my way of showing him I was becoming a man, as most, or maybe all young men feel they must do *in some form or fashion.* This was *my way* of getting my father to *back off* a little and begin to see me as a young adult *coming into my own.* That was truly a defining moment in my life! Daddy never said a word to me then or anytime thereafter regarding the matter. My mother told me he did, however, come to her later and ask, *"When the hell did that boy start smoking? He lit up a cigarette today in the truck, and I damn near drove off the road."* Let me mention that I quit smoking a few years later. It never really became a habit for me. It was just a fad. Oh, speaking of not knowing what my father might do, did I mention he also served as a part-time Police Officer in Brinkley?

# My Journey

**Introducing Officer Charlie J. Butler**

To my sons, grandchildren, and all who read this book, during that time, we did not know the dangers of smoking as we do now. It was glorified, and you never heard anything negative about it. We were never told it causes lung cancer, heart disease, strokes, and many other debilitating diseases. It was always advertised as the "cool" thing to do. So, to all who read this message, I pray that you never take up the habit of smoking. Do your own research.

## *BACK TO DADDY*

Daddy was very particular about how he looked. He wanted his clothes clean and neat, which meant my brothers and I had to do the ironing. We also had to keep his cars clean, even though he rarely let us take them out for a drive.

# My Journey

**SPECIAL NAMES**

Daddy had "Special Names" for the first five of his children he sometimes used when referring to us when he was angry. I don't think he meant to harm us by using these labels, but it behooves us as parents to be very careful about how we speak to our children because it could have a lasting negative effect on them. These labels daddy used when referring to us were very demeaning and demoralizing, and daddy would use them with such vitriol and anger in his voice.

Acy said he told mama he grew up being extremely afraid of daddy because of how he talked to him. Mama told Acy one of the reasons daddy expressed so much anger toward him was that he was afraid of Acy. During a recent discussion, Acy and I discussed the impact we think those labels may have had on some of us. Even though daddy referred to us in this manner, it should be noted that all of us truly loved our father, and I am sure he loved us just as much.

*Warning: I am trying to keep this autobiography honest and authentic. So, let me apologize now for any uncomfortable language some may feel is offensive. I'm just trying to keep it real!*

# My Journey

**Robert (Bobby) Was The "Ignorant Bastard."**

Daddy gave the impression that Bobby was not smart, so when he was angry at Bobby for something, he would refer to him as an "ignorant bastard." I think this had a negative effect on Bobby throughout his life.

As Bobby got older, he became much more reserved and quieter, and I wonder if it was because of the name-calling from daddy. Acy said because of daddy's reference to Bobby in this manner, he began to lack confidence and stopped speaking up in a crowd. He didn't feel like his opinion mattered.

Let me set the record straight, Bobby was intelligent and a wise decision-maker. Also, when he was in the military, he would write me letters and give me advice on different topics.

I looked forward to getting his letters and the guidance he would share with me about life, and things in general. I looked up to my big brother! I might also add that Bobby was a very good chess player, a thinking game. Bobby was also the best athlete in the family. He was always good at basketball, bowling, boxing, golf, billiards, etc.

# My Journey

**Acy Was The "Black Bastard."**

Daddy would often call Acy a black bastard because Acy's skin complexion was darker than the rest of us. Without a doubt, this negatively impacted Acy throughout his *entire* life. He recently shared with me he always felt inferior because of how daddy and his parents *(Big Mama and Big Daddy)* used to berate him and make him feel as if he was not as good as the rest of us. Acy said it was bad enough for daddy to constantly talk down to him and call him "a black bastard," but to make matters worse, when he was around our paternal grandparents, all three of them would attack him this way. He said he would also look at us and wonder why our skin complexion was lighter.

Sometimes when daddy was coming into the house from work, Acy would run and sit behind our wood-burning stove. Daddy would look for him and call out, "Acy Lee!" And then he would ask, "Where is that black bastard?" A heavy burden for a child to have to carry. Especially when it's your father, and sometimes your grandparents treating you this way.

It hurts me that this affected Acy so much. I've seen his pain over the years. He has even used "skin lighteners" on his skin. Acy told me before daddy died, he apologized to him for how he treated him when he was a child. He told Acy he was just an

# My Journey

ignorant father raised by ignorant parents, which was all he knew to do. I want you to know that my brother is, and has always been, a very handsome and intelligent dude. I have always admired my brother. As a young adult, I even tried to walk like him. I used to wish my personality was bold like his because I thought he was awesome!

**Lincoln Was The "Puny Bastard."**

Daddy called me Peter. I can still hear it as if it was yesterday, *"Peter, get your little ass somewhere and sit down before I beat the shit out of you! You little puny bastard."* I don't know why he called me a little puny bastard because as I stated before, I weighed 7 lbs. at birth. I even weighed more than Acy at birth. But I guess it was because I did not grow as fast as my other brothers, and consequently, they all grew up to be bigger than me.

Acy and I discussed this, and he said he sincerely believes daddy's reference to me as a "little puny bastard" was why I began lifting weights. He feels this was my way of showing others I was as big and tough as they were. I think he's spot-on with his assessment. As quiet as it's kept, I have often felt a little uncomfortable for usually being the smallest guy in a crowd.

# My Journey

Lifting weights gave me "the edge" I had never had because of my size.

After I began lifting weights, I was determined to outlift everybody who went up against me, and most times, I succeeded. Of course, I had an advantage over them. When they were sleeping at night, I was home in my garage training like a madman. As a result of all this hard training, I began to develop muscles everywhere and my body started changing. Not to mention the compliments I frequently got regarding my muscles, especially my arms. This made me begin to feel like a "big man!"

**Larry Was The "Big-Head Bastard."**

Daddy called Larry the big-head bastard because he felt like Larry's head was big for his body. Because of this constant reference, Larry started saying things like, *"Look at me, Look at me. I'm tough. I have a hard head. I can open the door with my head."* He would then proceed to run into the door headfirst and open it. He thought that was so funny, and at the time, we all did. I can hear daddy calling out to him now, "Larry, get in here! You little big-head bastard." I don't believe this had any long-term effects on Larry after we became adults. Ironically, Larry died at

# My Journey

the age of twenty-eight after losing control of a motorcycle and being thrown into a tree **Headfirst,** without a helmet!

**Brenda Was The "Bald Head Bastard."**

My parents' first four children were boys. Even though they wanted a girl, they just kept getting boys. Then, finally, on the fifth attempt, they successfully got the girl they had waited on for so long. But there was one little problem. She was born practically bald. As a result, mama and daddy started buying different types of grease and ointments to use on her head to get her hair to grow. Miraculously, it did begin to grow, and she eventually got a nice head of hair. But Brenda always liked to suck her finger on one hand and use the other hand to pull out her hair.

One day when Brenda was about two years old, daddy saw her sucking her finger and pulling on her hair and became very angry and called her a bald-headed bastard. That's when her name-calling began. As she got a little older, for whatever reason, she got some scissors and CUT HER HAIR OFF! My parents were livid! After all, they had spent the last couple of years doing everything they could to get her hair to grow. Not to mention they were spending money to buy chemicals for her hair they could have used to buy other things around the house. I remember daddy was so upset. He was fuming, and I think that's when he started back calling her a bald-headed bastard. Thankfully, Brenda doesn't remember this.

**PARENTS, BEWARE!**

You may be inflicting irreparable damage to your children with labeling and name-calling. Parents often resort to these cruel practices without thinking about how it makes the child feel or the negative and long-lasting impact it may have on them, such as withdrawal symptoms, self-destructive behavior *(drinking, drugs, etc.)*, anxiety, depression, and more.

So again, I encourage all parents to be cognizant of how you communicate with your children. You may be causing far-reaching and long-lasting damage to them without even realizing it.

**MORE INFORMATION ABOUT DADDY**

Overall, I recall daddy was very loyal to his parents and did the best he could for them. They were also very partial toward him because all their other children had moved "up north" or to Louisiana, but daddy stayed in Brinkley and was always there to help them when needed. As mentioned earlier, my father worked as a deliveryman for Dixie Furniture Company for most of his adult

## My Journey

life and earned an average of $110.00 bi-weekly. Daddy was crazy about his cars and made sure he always owned a decent vehicle. I also recall that my father spent a lot of his time "hanging out" in the streets, and I am certain he was spending money he could and should have used to help support his wife and children. In short, my "Papa Was a Rolling Stone!" ENOUGH SAID.

My father and my mother separated in December 1968. That's when my oldest brother Robert *(we called him Bobby)* and I went to Brinkley. We loaded up my mother and our six younger siblings and drove them to St. Louis, Missouri, where she resided for nearly five years.

*"When you look into your mother's eyes, you know that is the purest love you can find on this earth."* Mitch Albom

Cathryn Naomi (Williams) Butler

# My Journey

## MAMA

My mother's name is **Cathryn Naomi (Williams) Butler**. She was born February 12, 1925, to Mr. Tommie Williams and Mrs. Rowena (Hunt) Williams in a settlement west of Brinkley called **Hunt's Crossing**. Hunt's Crossing was named for mama's maternal grandfather because he owned so much of the land in that area. Mama died on October 23, 1990, while a patient at the University Hospital in Little Rock, Arkansas. The official cause of death was listed as renal failure.

## MEMORIES I HAVE OF MY MOTHER

Bobby, Acy, Larry, and I all grew up calling our mother "Lil' Ma," but I could not remember why. I asked Acy, and he informed me when Mama was pregnant with Bobby, Uncle Clarence started calling her "Lil' Ma." As a result, we *(her older kids)* called her Lil' Ma. After I met my wife, I noticed she called her parents "mama and daddy," and so I called them mama and daddy too.

For whatever reason, I decided if I were going to refer to Snow's parents as "mama and daddy," then I would start calling my own parents "mama and daddy." Acy said he could never break

# My Journey

the habit and called our parents "My Daddy and Lil' Ma" until they died. Mama was the most precious and nurturing mother any child could ever hope to have. She cared deeply for her children and "did without" to try to provide for our needs. She was in constant prayer for all of us. Her love for each of her children was endless. She was something special.

**BEST ADVICE FROM MAMA AS AN ADULT**

I remember living in Bronx, New York, at the time. And even though I was teaching school and working part-time at my brother-in-law's (Gaines) store in the evenings, it seemed like I never had much spare money. During one of my conversations with mama, I was complaining to her and questioning why I had even gone to college because it seemed like everyone in the family was making more money than me.

That's when mama spoke these prophetic words to me. She said, ***"Lincoln, it's not HOW MUCH you manage to make, it's how you manage WHAT you make!"*** This may be a small statement, but this little "nugget" has had a tremendous impact on how I handle my finances, and I have tried to govern my financial life accordingly ever since.

# My Journey

Mama shared with me that she only completed the 10$^{th}$ grade because it was the highest grade in the school at the time. She also informed me she only attended school about five months out of the year because she had to work on the farm the rest of the time. Even so, my mama was brilliant!

**MULTIPLE MYELOMA**

In 1985, my mother was diagnosed with Multiple Myeloma, a cancer that forms in a type of white blood cell called a plasma cell.

Mama bravely fought this disease for five years, spending time in the hospital and enduring various types of treatment. My sister, Brenda, was with me at the hospital when mama passed. I was on one side of her bed, and Brenda was on the other.

As mama was slowly fading away, we both talked to her and told her how much we loved her and that she had completed her work on this Earth. We told her we would all be okay because she had done an excellent job raising us. We told her it was okay to "let go" and be with God. In a few short moments, mama was gone. We were sad, but we could also rejoice because there was no more pain, no more agony, and no more suffering. To God be the Glory!

# My Journey

**MAMA'S INTERVIEW**

Prior to mama's death *(when her health had begun to improve)*, I went to Brinkley, and on Mother's Day, May 12, 1990. I conducted a video interview with mama about her life, and basically, nothing was off-limits. I will now share some of the highlights of that interview:

- Mama's Favorite Color: Blue
- Favorite Holiday: Christmas *(She said this was because more of her children come home during this time.)*
- Favorite Season: Spring
- Favorite Food: Greens, followed by Macaroni and Cheese
- Favorite Dessert: Chocolate Pie, followed by Banana Pudding and German Chocolate Cake

During the interview, I asked mama what the "Happiest Times of Her Life" were, and she sadly replied, *"Haven't had many!"* Wow, heartbreaking. I began thinking about all the "crap" she had to endure while living with daddy. Mama quickly added that she was always happy when her children came home.

She said, *"That's always a happy time!"* I then asked mama about the "Saddest Time of Her Life," and she replied, **"Losing Larry!"** My brother, Larry, was killed on a motorcycle across the street from my home at 2706 Whitewood Drive, Dallas, TX, on June 19, 1979. He was just 28 years old.

# My Journey

**Lawrence Larry Butler**
*(Deceased)*

The date was Tuesday, June 19, 1979. My wife was at work, and I was home with my three sons. That afternoon, my brother Larry, and his buddy Israel rode Israel's motorcycle over to my home to hang out. I was always happy to see my brother because we enjoyed each other's company. The three of us sat on my patio talking about grilling up some food for our wives before they got home from work. Here in Texas and other states, June 19th is a celebrated holiday.

According to my research, President Abraham Lincoln issued the Emancipation Proclamation on January 1, 1863, as the nation approached its third year of a bloody civil war. The proclamation declared *"that all persons held as slaves"* within the rebellious states *"are, and henceforward shall be free."* The news

# My Journey

of this proclamation did not reach Texas until June 19, 1865. Hence, that date is celebrated among African Americans. Ironically, since I began writing this autobiography, June 19th has been proclaimed a federally recognized holiday, thanks to the valiant efforts of Mrs. Opal Lee of Fort Worth, Texas. On June 17, 2021, President Joe Biden signed into law Senate Bill S. 475, making June 19th a Federal Holiday (Juneteenth).

While we sat there talking, the motorcycle became part of the conversation. Larry and Israel began explaining to me how to ride a motorcycle because I had never attempted to get on one alone. I remember Larry talking about how he rode them in the army. After more discussion and guidance, they convinced me to get on the bike and take my first solo ride. It was scary as I navigated the bike to the end of the street and turned around at the Wayland and Southwood Drives intersection. As soon as I returned to my driveway, Larry was waiting for me. He said, "I think I'll take a ride." My *three sons* were standing there, and after Larry got on the bike, he looked at them and asked, "Do one of you want to ride with me?" I looked at Larry and told him they could not go with him because I had never seen him ride a motorcycle before. I didn't want to take a chance at them getting hurt.

# My Journey

Sadly, and regrettably, I held the motorcycle up while my brother got on. He only traveled about 30-40 yards before hitting the curb on the left side of the street and crashing into a tree. After hitting the tree, he lost consciousness and never moved or made any sounds after we got to him. He died from head injuries. He was NOT wearing a helmet. Ironically, as he was getting on the motorcycle, out of concern, I asked him, "Larry, can you handle it?"

That's when he turned to me, revved up the engine, and then uttered his last words: ***"I'll be okay, Linc."*** He then sped off and crashed immediately into the tree. He never had control of the bike. I remember his last words because, on the day of his funeral, one of my sons wrote this on his copy of the obituary: "Larry's last words, I'll be okay, Linc." My brother, Acy, saw this and brought the obituary to me. Like my mother, "**Larry's death was also the saddest day of my life!**"

I rode in the ambulance with my brother to Methodist Hospital on Colorado Boulevard and watched the Paramedics work feverishly trying to resuscitate him. When we got to the emergency dock, some of the hospital staff were waiting and quickly escorted me to the registration desk to provide information they needed on Larry.

# My Journey

As I answered their questions, I noticed this priest on the other side of the wall constantly peeking at me from around the corner of the wall. I didn't know it at the time, but Larry had expired on the way to the hospital, and the priest was waiting for me to complete the registration process so he could inform me that Larry had passed. I was extremely nervous and had this strange feeling, and when they asked me for his birthdate, I just knew he had died and began to cry.

About that time, the priest stepped around the corner and asked me to accompany him to this little private room. I immediately stopped in my tracks and asked him, "Is my brother dead?" He looked me in the eyes and said, "Yes, he's dead." I then asked him very emphatically, "Are you telling me that my brother has NO life left in his body?" Again, the priest said, "Yes, he's dead." He then took me into the room and tried to comfort me. I remember telling him I was going to be okay. I told him I was only thinking about how this would affect my mother. I remember saying, "This is going to kill my mother."

Shortly afterward, my sister Linda, and her husband, Paul, arrived at the hospital. After we consoled each other for a few minutes, we devised a plan to break this tragic news to mama. I did not want mama to find out by way of a phone call, and I did not

# My Journey

want her to be alone when she got the news. I also did not want my sisters and brothers to find out before mama because they would immediately start calling her.

So, I asked Linda and Paul to drive to Brinkley, then go next door to Uncle Robert's house and get him to go to mama's house with them. Uncle Robert and Paul were ministers, so I thought this would help. I told Linda to call me from Uncle Robert's house just as they were preparing to go next door to mama's house so I could call the rest of our brothers and sisters.

I was awake all night trying to process what had happened and wondered if and how we would get through this. I don't know if I briefly fell asleep during the night, but I distinctly saw a *calming light* over my bed. There was nothing said aloud, but I had this STRONG feeling inside of me that Larry was staring at me. As I said, no words were spoken, but I clearly sensed him saying, *"I'm okay Linc! Don't worry about me. I'm okay!"* That was a very long and painful night for me. I felt like I had let my brother down because I was the "big brother" who was supposed to come to Dallas and pave the way for him.

*Over the years, I have experienced many, many emotions because of this tragedy. It is truly difficult for me to explain how much this affected my life. I still miss him so much.* You see, mama

# My Journey

had paired us all up: Acy and Bobby were a pair, Larry and I were a pair, Morris and Stanley were a pair, and our three sisters had each other.

Even though I was more than three years older than Larry, he was like my twin and was very protective of me. He once drove from Flint, MI, to Brinkley, AR, on a Sunday to check on me. *(That's about an eleven-hour one-way trip.)* I was in my first year of teaching and was the only sibling still living in Brinkley.

My parents had already moved away. I was shocked and surprised to see him because I had no idea he was coming. I asked him what in the world he was doing in Brinkley on a Sunday evening. He said, *"Linc, I had a dream that someone was messing with you, so I had to come and make sure you were okay!"* I said, *"Larry Butler, that's what the telephone is for."* He said, *"Yeah, I know, but I just wanted to see for myself."* That's just how loving and protective he was.

One of the cars Larry owned at the time of his death was a Green Volkswagen. During that time, I experienced severe migraine headaches. Often, Larry would stop by after I got home from work or on the weekends to see if I wanted to "hang out" for a while. No matter how bad my head was hurting, if I heard that Volkswagen pulling up in my driveway, I immediately perked up

# My Journey

and was ready to ride with my brother. Snow would give me *that look* and say, *"I thought you had a bad headache!"* I can't explain it, but Larry just had a wonderful effect on me. When he showed up, it felt like everything was going to be okay.

I must tell this story as well. The year was 1975. I was still living in New York but had started considering moving to Dallas. Larry was back in Flint, Michigan, on leave from the army. I decided to go to Flint and spend some time with him before he reported back for duty. While we were in Flint, Larry said he did not want to live in Flint when he got out of the army. As I stated, I was already planning to move to Dallas the next year, so we began our discussion about us both moving to Texas. I remember telling Larry since I was going to get to Dallas before him, I would go and *pave the way*. We were both excited about the idea of moving to Dallas.

I arrived in Dallas in October 1976, and Larry got here during the summer of 1977. However, he did not come straight to Dallas. Instead, he went to Opelousas, Louisiana, to spend time with his wife and her family. I was disappointed because I wanted him to come to Dallas first. Larry said, *"Come on, Linc, I have to go see my wife first!"* Shame on me. I had a lot of nerve wanting him to come here where I was before going to see his wife.

## My Journey

Anyway, I didn't want to wait those few weeks before seeing him, so I got in my car and drove to Opelousas, Louisiana, to spend some time with him. Now, some may say that I was insane, but that is just how I felt about my brother!

I stayed in Louisiana for a few days, and while there, we drove to New Orleans, hung out for a day and night, and had a great time. I then drove back to Dallas and waited for Larry to move here. Larry arrived in Dallas a few weeks later and stayed with me until he got his own place. That made me about as happy as a man could be. Man, I loved my brother and loved being in his company. A short time later, Larry's wife joined him in Dallas.

**BACK TO MAMA'S INTERVIEW**

In the meantime, I began asking mama if there was *any place* she once thought about visiting but never had the chance. I asked her if there was any *special gift* item she wanted or thought she would like to own. *Whatever place mama would have wanted to visit or whatever special gift she may have liked, I WAS GOING TO MAKE THAT HAPPEN! (I had already given her some fine jewelry, a car, etc. I did my best to provide for mama as well as possible with the little money I made.)* But mama told me she never really wanted a lot of things and there was no place she would like to visit now. She said she just wanted to be comfortable in the time

## My Journey

she had left. When I asked mama if she had any fears, she said she feared death. I remember telling her I don't want to suffer in any way, but I don't really fear death.

Mama then told me how she felt when she decided to move to St. Louis. She said *moving to St. Louis was the hardest decision she had ever made in her life.* It was in the cold of winter, January 1969, when mama asked Bobby and me to drive her to St. Louis to stay with her brother, Uncle Clarence, and his wife, Annie B., a.k.a. "Aunt Bee."

Uncle Clarence & Aunt Bee

Mama indicated that life had become unbearable at home with daddy. She also stated that she had begun to fear him because

# My Journey

of the way he started behaving and the verbal abuse she was enduring. She said he started acting like this after her older children had left home. *(I guess he knew my older brothers and I would not sit by quietly and allow mama to be verbally abused.)*

Leaving daddy was not a spontaneous or spur-of-the-moment decision for mama. No, she had planned everything and informed us exactly when to show up at our home in Brinkley on that cold morning. She wanted us to arrive after daddy had left home for work so she could leave without any drama! Bobby and I were away at college in Pine Bluff, Arkansas.

Thankfully, daddy was at work when we arrived, so we loaded everybody up and left without incident. Mama had also solicited the help of one of our cousins, Willie Johnson, a.k.a. **Bare Bran.** We used his car because we needed two cars to carry all the children and the clothes. As we headed down the highway for St. Louis, mama mentioned how scary it was to go to an unfamiliar city with eight of her children *(five would be staying in St. Louis with her).* In my interview with mama, she stated that she only had $7.00 to her name when she arrived in St. Louis. She never let any of us know this at the time.

During the trip to St. Louis, we had to deal with a lot of snow and cold weather, and I became very sick with strep throat. I

## My Journey

had to see a doctor that evening after arriving in St. Louis. A couple of days or so after getting mama settled in St. Louis, Bobby and I returned to Pine Bluff to resume our college studies. *(We did make a brief stop in Brinkley but did not see daddy, so we went on to Pine Bluff.)*

Shortly after mama had moved to St. Louis, she was notified by her sisters back in Brinkley that daddy had moved his woman into her house. Mama was furious and wrote me a letter stating how angry she was. She said she had bought a gun and if we could not get them out of her house, she would come down there and do it herself! After carefully reading the letter, I went and found Bobby, and without saying a word, I handed the letter to him.

When Bobby finished reading the letter, he looked at me and simply said, "You ready to go?" I said, "Let's go!" We jumped in my car and headed for Brinkley. The trip to Brinkley from Pine Bluff is about 80 miles and takes approximately one and a half hours. I doubt if we said three or four words during that entire trip. We were in deep concentration because mama had spoken clearly, and we were on our way to "handle our business," daddy or no daddy. The bottom line, they were going to have to GO!

God knew what was best and I am grateful they had already moved out because it would probably have been an ugly scene.

## My Journey

Somehow, daddy had gotten the word a few days before our arrival that Mama was sending us there to put them out. So, I guess he decided to avoid the drama and quickly moved out of the house before we got there. Months later, my father loaded up his *new* family and moved to Chicago. After the *dust had settled,* I began visiting my father in Chicago, and I must say, I enjoyed spending time with him.

Over the years, mama often talked about how helpful and supportive Uncle Clarence and Aunt Bee were to her and her children while she was in St. Louis. She appreciated their love, support, encouragement, and kindness. She also talked about how well her kids and Uncle Clarence's kids got along and how they often took up for each other.

During my interview with mama, I asked her if she had any advice for her grandchildren and great-grandchildren. This is what she said:

- Get a good education because you are going to need it.
- Have a good Christian upbringing; she encouraged us to teach them about God because He is a higher power to call on.
- Teach them to work and stand on their own.

The video recording of mama's interview has proved to be priceless! Sometimes I pull out my DVD and watch it, and I am so

## My Journey

grateful to hear mama's voice and see her as she was. Glory be to God! *(I transferred the recording from VHS to DVD and gave copies to each of my siblings.)*

I mentioned earlier that mama spent time in the hospital being treated for her cancer, and at times, she was very, very ill. Here is a picture taken in 1989 during one of mama's hospital stays:

**Mama at the University Hospital with all her children.**

SPECIAL SCRAPBOOK FOR MAMA

My sisters constructed and designed a scrapbook representing our families. Some of us included a written message to mama about what she meant to us. Here are some of the pictures, letters, and messages we wrote to mama and included in the scrapbook. We presented the scrapbook to her in November 1989.

# My Journey

Our mother was beautiful inside and out, and she loved, prayed, and cared for her children to the very end. See the "Prayer" below that I firmly believe was written on Monday, October 1, 1990, the day I signed the contract and closed on mama's new home that Snow and I were helping to buy.

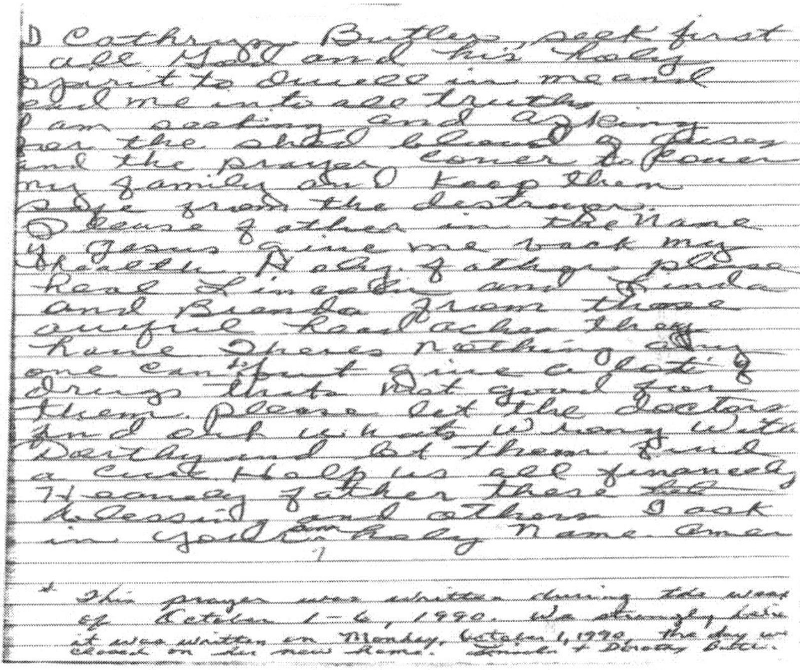

*[Handwritten prayer, partially legible:]*

> Catherine Butler, seek first all God and His Holy Spirit to dwell in me and lead me into all truth. I am seeking and applying the shed blood of Jesus and the prayer cover to cover my family and keep them safe from the destroyer. Please Father in the Name of Jesus, give me back my real Lin, Cathi, and give Real Lin relief and Brenda from those awful headaches they have. There's nothing one can't but give a lot of drugs that do not give free of them. Please let the doctors find out what is wrong with Dorothy and let them find a cure. Help us all financially Heavenly Father, these blessings and others I ask in Your Holy Name. Amen.

*This prayer was written during the week of October 1-6, 1990. We strongly believe it was written on Monday, October 1, 1990, the day we closed on the new home. Snow & Dorothy Butler.*

After "closing" on mama's house, I will never forget the experience my siblings and I had while moving mama's furniture and all her belongings to the "new house." Remember, mama was

# My Journey

still in the hospital in Little Rock, but it seemed like every 15-20 minutes she would call me on the phone and ask where we had placed a particular piece of furniture.

I would let her know we had placed the item where she had instructed. She would then say, *"It fit in that space, didn't it?"* I would tell her yes, it fit well in that spot! She would then say, *"I knew it would fit because I had already gone up there and measured where I wanted everything to go!"*

Mama was excited as we moved different items to her new home. But there was one little problem. Mama kept calling me and interrupting our work. Finally, I told mama we would never finish moving her things if she didn't stop calling us so often.

Mama was so happy, and I was happy and excited for her. Sadly, mama passed away twenty-two days later, on October 23, 1990. She was still in the hospital in Little Rock and never got a chance to live in her new home. My mother was only 65 years old.

# My Journey

**MAMA'S NEW HOME!!! That's my car in the driveway.**

In the next chapter, I share some information from the scrapbook compiled by my siblings, from the oldest to the youngest. I am so glad we wrote these letters and messages to mama because sometimes we get so busy living our own lives, we forget to let the most important people know how much they mean to us. We tend to take for granted they will be here forever. I am so grateful we were able to share the scrapbook with mama while she still lived.

NOTE: As you look at the pictures and messages, remember these were placed in her scrapbook back in 1989. That's why you don't

## My Journey

see any recent pictures in this section. These are the exact pictures from her book.

# My Journey

## Chapter IV: Content from Mama's 1989 Scrapbook

**Robert (Bobby) L. Butler, Sr.**

Robert was born on April 14, 1944, in Brinkley, Arkansas *(actually, it was in Hunt's Crossing)* and died on March 19, 2020, in Dallas, Texas. He was 75 years old. He did not write a personal message but included some beautiful pictures of his family for mama to enjoy. *These are just a couple of the photos from the scrapbook.*

# My Journey

Barbara, Rochelle, Robert, Sr.
Robert, Jr., Betty, Emeka

Jeanette Atkins
(Bobby's 1st Born)

**Acy L. Butler, Sr.**

Acy was born on February 8, 1946, in Brinkley, Arkansas *(actually, it was in Hunt's Crossing)*. Acy did not write a personal message but included some beautiful pictures of his family for mama to enjoy. *These are just a couple of the photos from the scrapbook.*

# My Journey

Acy and Carolyn Butler

Paula, Acy Jr., Donna    Monte, Antoine, Paula

**Lincoln Butler, Sr.**

Lincoln was born on September 12, 1947, in Toledo, Ohio.

# My Journey

Lincoln & Dorothy Butler
Sons: Michael, Lincoln Jr., Dirrick

Lincoln

I want to share a letter I presented to mama along with some family pictures. I wrote the letter to mama to express my love and admiration for her as a great mom.

*Dear Mom,*

*I just want you to know how much I love and admire you. You are truly the epitome of God's ideal woman and mother. You exhibit such courage, dignity, wisdom, and strength, even in times of distress. Last year when I visited you in the hospital, I was so scared, but I didn't want you to know it. I found my strength in you and in God. You handled everything so well and that helped all of us.*

*While I will never have all the things I want in this life, I must say I feel extremely rich and blessed because of your divine*

# My Journey

*love. If you have ever wondered what your children think of you as a mother, let me tell you, we think you are truly the BEST! You are #1 in our book.*

*Mama, I have always tried to live my life so you could be proud of me.* ***I only hope I have made you as proud to be my mother as I am to be your son.*** *Forever know that I love you, and I thank God He blessed me with a beautiful mother like you. Forever with love,*

*Lincoln Butler, Sr.*

Lincoln Butler, Sr. (Butler #3)


**Lawrence Larry Butler**

Larry was born December 6, 1950, in Brinkley, Arkansas *(in the house where the Banks family lived)* and died June 19, 1979, in Dallas, Texas. He was only 28 years old. Here's a letter from Larry *(written by my sisters)* that was presented to mama in the scrapbook.

# My Journey

Larry & Brenda					Larry, Brenda & Taisha

# My Journey

Lawrence Larry Butler

*To My Dear Mom and Dad,*

*Although I can't be with you today physically, I am with you in spirit. Thank you, mom, for being the best friend and mother anyone could have. Dad, I wish we could have had more time together, but thank God for the time we did have.*

*To My Brothers and Sisters,*

*Love one another and be good to each other. Take care of one another and be good to your families. Always honor our father and mother. God is smiling on our family. Pray for one another as I am praying for you that we will all be together again: ONE GREAT BIG HAPPY FAMILY where there will be no more sorrow and no more pain, just joy, peace, and happiness.*

*Love, Larry*

# My Journey

**Brenda Kay (Butler) Morrison**

Brenda was born on **April 29, 1953,** in Brinkley, Arkansas.

Luther, Brenda, Kim, Luther,Jr.          Brenda and Gussie *(cousin)*

Taken from the scrapbook, this is a letter that Brenda wrote to mama:

# My Journey

*November 20, 1989*

*Dear Mommy,*

*Roses are Red, Violets are Blue. I love you and I know that you love me too! During the years that you raised us, I know that it could not have been easy, but you smiled and never complained. You just kept cleaning, cooking, teaching, sometimes even preaching, praying, doing without, and trusting in God Almighty to see you through.*

*Thanks be to GOD: You, are my mom. I'm sure there were times when you weren't always pleased with the way I may have handled situations, but you gave your advice, stepped back, and let me experience life as I had to do. Thanks for knowing what to say, how to say it, and when to say it. You're the greatest, mom. I cannot thank God enough because had it not been for you and Him, I would not be the person I am today.*

*I love you,* Brenda

# My Journey

## William Morris Butler

William was born June 7, 1956, in Brinkley, Arkansas.

Erma, William, Takela      William

Morris wrote this to mama in the scrapbook:

### *A Mother's Love*

*There are things in life that cannot be simulated.
Among these things lies a mother's love.
It is the light that conveys a new day,
A universal sensation that guides all living creatures.
It is as strong as the scent of
spring flowers during a passionless winter.
It is as unpredictable as the future
Yet as clear as the present.
And if a father's love is a majestic peacock feather,
Then surely a mother's love is the peacock.
It is an eternal waterfall
Emanating to the depths of our hearts.
Sometimes we might question but should never doubt.
A Mother's Love.
Mama, I love you very much.
Your son,
Morris*

# My Journey

**Stanley Butler**

Stanley was born on April 23, 1959, in Brinkley, Arkansas.

Stanley                    Tiffany & Ricky

**This is what Stan wrote to mama:**

*Mama, I just want to say thank you not only for giving me life, but also for serving as an example of how to live this life. I have been through a lot of tough times thus far in my short years. Undoubtedly, you are the main reason I have come through these tough times and will get through whatever else life throws my way. Through your trust and belief in God, it has allowed me to keep my faith. I thank you for your prayers and I thank God for*

## My Journey

*His many blessings. I thank Him for giving me the most precious gift in the world, Cathryn N. Butler, for my mother. I am so proud of you that I could burst. You've been through tough times all your life, but you continue to maintain that wonderful smile.*

*I want to thank you for giving me your blessings when I decided to get married at such a young age and to someone who was still in high school. I know that wasn't easy for you to do. But with your blessings and God's will, we have been together for nearly ten years. Thanks for your prayers during my bout with drugs. I promise you, with God's help, that you will <u>never</u> have to worry in that way about me again. I love you.*

*P. S. Thank God for this wonderful treasure you have given me and my brothers and sisters. (Our Mom)*

*Stan Butler*

# My Journey

**Linda (Butler) Pighee**

Linda was born on April 20, 1960, in Brinkley, Arkansas.

Gary, Linda, Paul                    Linda

This is what Linda wrote to mama:

### *MOTHER*

*Mother is a caring, sharing, giving, and loving person.*
*Mother taught me right from wrong before I was grown.*
*Mother taught me what I needed to know before I had to go.*
*Mother bounced me on her knee, thank God I know she prayed for me.*
*Mother said if I trust God as I should, it all will work out for my good.*

# My Journey

*Mother, you held my hand as a child only for a while, but when I had to depart, you forever held my heart.*

*Mother sacrificed many things she needed, so I could have some of the things I wanted.*

*Mother, thank you for this special love you so graciously passed on to your children.*

*For there is but one other greater love than that of a Mother's Love.*

*Linda*

Linda (Butler) Pighee

## Kathy Ann (Butler) Franklin

Kathy was born on May 30, 1962, in Brinkley, Arkansas.

Kathy

Kathy, Benny, Lawrence

# My Journey

## This is what Kathy wrote to mama:

*Words or pictures could never express the love I feel for you. When God created woman, he must have had you in mind, because in my heart, you're one of a kind. I've always loved you and always will. But I didn't fully understand the love you had for me until you set me free. I've grown up in so many ways and often think of the things you taught me when I was there. The values you have; the morals we share. I love you more with each passing day and I thank God for giving us one more day.*

*Now, the Lord has blessed me with children of my own. I pray to God that I may be as good a mom as you've*

## My Journey

*been to me. I pray for guidance in all that I do and hope they love me as I love you.*

*When you are down and trouble comes your way, count your blessings, and remember the love God has for you. He blessed you with ten beautiful children all of whom love you.*

*Kathy*

Kathy

# My Journey

Until mama left Brinkley for St. Louis, she worked as a maid cleaning the homes of some of the more affluent White families in town. Sometimes she worked two jobs in one day, leaving one home and going to the other to repeat the same cleaning chores.

After completing these domestic chores, she would then have to come home and prepare dinner for us while also having to deal with my father after he got home from "hanging out." My mother was paid, on average, $2.00 a day. If I recall correctly, sometimes she received $2.50 per day. UNBELIEVABLE! But she did what she had to do to try to take care of her children!

After moving to St. Louis, mama worked at Barnes Hospital and barely made enough to take care of her children. Here is a copy of her employment information at Barnes Hospital, dated 5/25/70, showing that she was paid $1.85 per hour. (8 hrs. x 1.85 =

# My Journey

$14.80 per day x 5 days = $74.00 weekly) My God, I didn't know Mama was struggling like this because she never let us know. I found this document after mama died. This truly breaks my heart.

Mama stayed in St. Louis for more than four years, and then the time came in 1974 when she decided she was ready to move back to Brinkley, Arkansas. I lived in New York City then, and I didn't want mama to move back to Brinkley without a car. Since Daddy was no longer living with the family, I knew having a car to go back home in would mean a lot to mama and my younger siblings. They were growing up and coming into their own as teenagers. I had paid off my 1969 Mercury Montego and decided to give it to mama to go back home.

I did not tell mama ahead of time. She thought I was coming to St. Louis to visit them before they moved back to Brinkley. I remember leaving New York one afternoon, and by the time I got to Pennsylvania, my radiator burst. I was stranded alone on the highway until finally, I flagged down a state trooper.

After I explained my problem to him, he called me a tow truck and the driver towed me to a repair shop in the nearest town. Unfortunately, when we got there, everything had closed for the night. The tow truck driver told me he knew some people out in the

# My Journey

country who could fix the radiator for me. He called them, and they told him to bring me out there.

The driver towed me down a long dark road out in the countryside. I was alone without any protection on me, but I was never really afraid. When he got me to the farmhouse, there were three or four "ole-timers" with long beards sitting around outside the barn. The men greeted me and were very friendly. Then they asked me to "pop the hood." After I released the hood latch, I remember the men laughing while I removed the chain.

*Living in New York City, we had to keep our hoods "chained" so no one could get under our hood and steal the battery or anything else they wanted.* The men thought that was the craziest thing they had ever seen. They asked me all sorts of questions about life in New York City. After some time had passed, they repaired the radiator and I was on my way back to the expressway.

I was glad to be back in civilization. Honestly, I enjoyed spending time with those men telling them about life in the big city and listening to them talk about their life in a small, rural town out in the country. Oh, did I mention they were all White men? But they were extremely nice and hospitable.

# My Journey

Now that I was safely back on the highway, I continued my journey to St. Louis. All along the way, I thought about how I would present the Montego to mama and let her know it now belonged to her. Mama knew how much I loved that Montego! It was the first new car I had ever owned.

**MY SPECIAL GIFT FOR MAMA**

Finally, after arriving in St. Louis, I recall spending a little time talking to everyone and then asking mama and the family to step outside because I wanted to show them something in the car. As I walked over to the Montego with mama, I remember telling her I did not want her to walk to get around town and attend church when she got back to Brinkley. I told her how much I loved her and then said, *"Mama, from my heart (pointing at my heart), I give my heart (pointing at the car), to my heart (pointing at mama while handing her the keys to the Montego)!"*

The look on mama's face was PRICELESS! She said, "Lincoln, what are you saying?" And I said, "Mama, the Montego is fully paid for, and it now belongs to you!"

Mama said, "What are you going to do for a car?" I then reassured mama I had purchased another car which was in New

# My Journey

York and I would be flying back there in a couple of days. Mama was so happy and grateful.

Being able to do that for my mother and my younger siblings meant the world to me because there was no daddy around to help them in this way. By the way, I don't remember what the reaction was from my brothers and sisters, but I am sure they were extremely happy as well!

This is **MY very own Mercury Montego** that I gave to Mama.

**Enjoying a weekend in Windsor, Canada, in 1971**

I stayed in St. Louis for a couple of days with mama and my younger siblings before returning to New York.

# My Journey

## MY SIBLINGS' DESCRIPTIONS OF EACH OTHER

*Last year, I asked each of my siblings to list two-three positive things that describe something special or unique about each other. Without any reference to who said what, these are the descriptions from all the brothers and sisters:*

**Robert "Bobby" Butler, Sr.** (April 14, 1944 - March 19, 2020) He was an athletic and kind big brother who was strong and easy-going. He was also humble and set the foundation for the rest of us as a good example of who we should be as brothers and sisters in this family. He was loving and raised the bar in setting a high example of dignity and respect for our children and grandchildren. In the early years he was very talkative. He talked all the time, and never shut up. But he had a good heart, and he was a good boxer with an awesome smile. He was resilient, soft-spoken and had a beautiful spirit.

**Acy L. Butler, Sr.** (February 8, 1946) – He is adventurous, inquisitive, courageous, daring, bold, brave, and strong. At the same time, he is caring, loving, generous, and laid back. He is a big brother who loves to the detriment of his own well-being. He literally will go without to help others. He loves people without judging them. He is a smart, spiritual, determined pilgrim passing

# My Journey

through. His free spirit and risk-taking personality make him complex. But he is always looking out for us.

**Lincoln Butler, Sr.** (September 12, 1947) – His precise, thorough and punctual attitude allows him to think and plan, making him a strong leader and mentor. He is a giving, loving and protective man who is dedicated to family. He is task-oriented, making him the ultimate professional. He is a mentor who is an educator-4-life. Growing up he did his own thing and had his own friends, but he was always there.

**Lawrence "Larry" Butler** (December 6, 1950 – June 19, 1979) *Died on Daddy's Birthday* – He was a protective, caring, fun-loving, big-hearted, loveable, and free-spirited soul. He was so understanding that the ladies loved him. Larry could have had his own reality show · because he experienced life to the fullest. But as much as he loved life, he loved us more. He had your back! Big brother, I miss you ·

**Brenda (Butler) Morrison** (April 29, 1953) – She is a kind, loving and caring big sis who loves her family unconditionally. Her compassion allows her to forgive easily. She is a prayer warrior whose bond with our Lord and Savior is unbreakable. She is an expert on the joy of preparing and

# My Journey

consuming interesting cuisine (food)⋯. She is also a a very good gardener.

**Lawrence Wilbur Butler** (June 19, 1955-June 21, 1955) – He only lived 1½ days, but he is loved and never forgotten. Although he is an angel in heaven, he was lost potential here on earth. *(Born on Daddy's Birthday)*

**William Morris Butler, Sr.** (July 7, 1956) – He is a dependable, strong, caring man. His determination to never change his beliefs has served him amazingly well as a big brother, husband, father and grandfather. This consistency makes him stand tall as a gentle giant whose kindness is felt in everything he does.

**Stanley Butler** (April 23, 1959) – Family gatherings brighten up when Stan shows up *(with his quarters-smile). His* fun-loving attitude makes him the life of the party. He's also intelligent, strong, and resilient, and never gives up without a fight! This makes him resourceful. The love and support of his family increase his determination. He is blessed ⋅.

**Linda (Butler) Pighee** (April 20, 1960) – She is very creative, smart, and down to earth. She is so easy to talk to about complex issues. Her passion is evident, especially when it comes to her political opinions. Her creativity shines through in her

# My Journey

crafting. Her love of family and her sweet, sensitive spirit makes everyone believe she has the favor of God.

**Kathy Ann (Butler) Franklin** (May 30, 1962) – She is extremely generous with her finances and time, giving advice, support and mentorship. She is our north star who is loving, sweet, and wise beyond her years. She is that best friend who will do anything for her brothers and sisters. And she will speak her mind!

NOTE: It is truly a blessing and an honor to be a member of this wonderful, loving family. Reading the descriptions that each sibling wrote warms my heart. We are indeed a family that loves each other! Thank you, mama, for raising us this way.

Front Row L to R: (Sisters) – Kathy, Linda, Brenda

# My Journey

Back Row L to R: (Brothers) – Stanley, William "Morris" Lincoln, Acy, Robert "Bobby" *(Deceased)*

# My Journey

## Chapter V: Grandparents, Special Uncles and Aunts

### MEMORIES OF MY PATERNAL GRANDPARENTS

Mr. Andrew Butler, Sr.
(Big Daddy)

Mrs. Curlie Butler
(Big Mama)

My grandfather's name is Andrew Butler, Sr. *(We called him Big Daddy.)*. He was born in Monroe, Louisiana March 15, 1894. He died in 1973 in Fargo,

# My Journey

Arkansas. My grandmother's name is Curlie Scott Butler *(We called her Big Mama.)* Big Mama was born on November 28, 1897, in Baydale, Arkansas. She died May 17, 1985, in Chicago, Illinois. Before moving to Memphis, Tennessee, they lived in Baton Rouge, Monroe, and Chapel Hill, Louisiana. They later moved to Fargo, Arkansas, in the mid-thirties.

After moving to Fargo, Acy said they worked as "sharecroppers" for White people and eventually were able to purchase over 40 acres of land. Apparently, my grandparents did well because it is a known fact that sharecroppers did not profit much from this arrangement. Therefore, to purchase and hold on to this much land, my grandparents must have really done a good job saving their money.

Both of my grandparents were extremely hard-working and very industrious people. I remember as a youngster, seeing how hard Big Daddy worked and thinking, "That is a working little ole man." Big Daddy farmed almost all his 40 acres of land. He and Big Mama basically did all the work themselves. He worked from sun up to sun down and planted cotton, corn, potatoes, watermelons, peanuts, etc. His farm had hogs, chickens, horses, and cows. He owned a car and truck. He also had lots of farm

# My Journey

equipment to do the work. Big Daddy was somewhat quiet and reserved, but he was *"tough as nails!"*

Big Mama was part Native American. As a youngster, I remember watching her dye her hair black and thinking how much she resembled the Native Americans we had seen on TV. She was more outspoken and more opinionated than Big Daddy.

She never had a problem expressing her feelings and telling you what was on her mind. Whenever daddy was at their home in Fargo fussing about something, you could always count on Big Mama joining in and supporting daddy. Big Mama worked alongside Big Daddy on their farm, no matter the chore.

I remember her working in the cotton fields, feeding chickens, and milking cows. I watched her ring the necks of chickens before dropping them in a bucket of hot water. She then pulled their feathers out before preparing them for cooking.

I enjoyed the big country meals she prepared for us. After our dinner, I remember playing in the haystack in the barn on a few occasions. I had fun on their farm when I was not working in the cotton fields.

# My Journey

## MEMORIES OF MY MATERNAL GRANDPARENTS

**Mrs. Rowena Hunt Williams & Mr. Tommie Williams**

(a.k.a. Big Mama & Papa)

Big Mama's parents were Alfred and Amanda Hunt. They were upper-middle-class Blacks from Dyersburg, Tennessee. They moved to Arkansas and bought a large spread of land west of Brinkley around the turn of the century (1880-1896). In fact, they owned so much of the land that a small township was formed and named after them. Hence the name: **Hunt's Crossing**.

Papa was born on March 24, 1876, and died on December 12, 1957. He was a very kind and soft-spoken man. I don't ever remember Papa working anywhere. I just remember him sitting on the front porch a lot. Acy said he has never heard anyone talking

# My Journey

about Papa working either. He said Papa used to wear an old army jacket and would stand on the side of the house to get some sun.

When I was a young boy, Papa wanted me to go to the store for him. The store was only a few blocks from the house with only two roads to take. There was a mean kid along the route on both roads. On the front road was a tough kid named Maine Scott, and on the other road was a kid named Raymond Clay. I couldn't get to the store without passing one of them.

These kids never fought with me, but they had a reputation for jumping on kids who passed their homes. So, I was very hesitant to go to the store alone that day. When I mentioned this to Papa, he reminded me to try to live my life so that others won't have a reason to want to harm me in any way. Really! A lot of good that did me. I'm thinking, *"I need some real help right now."* I went on to the store that day without incident. I never forgot Papa's words of advice on living your life in a way to avoid conflict.

Big Mama was born on October 2, 1882, in Dyersburg, Tennessee, and died from a stroke on April 13, 1963, in Brinkley, Arkansas. She was eighty-one at the time of her death. Big Mama was an assertive, strong, and very loving person with a full head of gray hair. She was the enforcer and handled most things around the

# My Journey

house. She was known for getting the switch out when her grandchildren misbehaved.

In fact, many times the grandchildren had to go and get their own switch. I can still hear her saying, "Go get me a switch so I can whip you." Big Mama was a "midwife" and delivered many babies in and around that area. She and Papa also held weekly Bible study sessions in their home for the grandchildren and some adults. They were good, strong, hard-working Christians who were loved by many.

Almost all the acreage Big Mama's parents left them was squandered and pillaged away. One story has it that Papa sold about fifteen acres of his land for a "Top Hat" and a pair of shoes, not knowing that he was giving away so much of his land. Before he died, he sold the rest of the land and bought lots *(homesites)* for each of his children to build or occupy houses, mainly around the Brinkley area and mostly on the "**West End**." It is said he divided the remaining money between his children.

*NOTE: Some of this information about my grandparents was taken from our family history documents researched by my nephew, Ramon Pighee, and cousin, Louis Terrell Sanders.*

# My Journey

**Interview with Mrs. Rowena Williams *(Big Mama)* – 1938**

**This is my mother's mother.**

My Nephew, Ramon Pighee, found this article from 1938 while researching on Ancestry.

Ramon wrote:

*"I found this from an interview on Ancestry with Rowena Williams conducted in 1938 when she was 56 years old. She was born in 1882. Apparently, in the mid-30s, a group of people sought out the former slaves before they all died and interviewed them. The print on ancestry wasn't great quality unless you were looking at it in the app (so it wasn't worth trying to copy and send). As it turns out, I was able to find a print on the net and have copied it below:"*

Interviewer: Miss Irene Robertson
Person Interviewed: Rowena Hunt Williams
R.F.D., **Brinkley, Arkansas**
Age: 56

"My mother was Amanda McVey. She was born two years, six months after freedom in Corinth, Mississippi. My father was born in slavery. Grandma lived with us at her death. Her name was Emily McVey. She was sold in her girlhood days. Uncle George was sold to a man in the settlement named Lee. His name was Joe Lee (Lea?). Another of my uncles was sold to a man named Washington. His name was George Washington. They were sold at

# My Journey

*different times. Being sold was their biggest dread. Some of them wanted to be sold trusting to be treated better.*

*"Mother and grandma didn't have a hard time like my father said he come up under. He said he was brought up hard. He was raised (reared) at Jackson, Tennessee. He was never sold. Master Alf Hunt owned him and his young master, Willie Hunt, inherited him. He said they never put him in the field till he was twelve years old. He started ploughing a third part of a day.*

*A girl about grown and another boy a little older took turns to do a 'buck's' (a grown man) work. They was lotted of a certain tract and if it stay clear they had a certain time to get it all done. He said they got whooped and half fed. When the War was on, his white folks had to half feed their own selves. He talked like if the War had lasted much longer it would been a famine in the land. He hit this world in time to have a hard time of it. After freedom was worse time in his life.*

*"In August when the crops was laid, Master Hunt called them to the house at one o'clock by so many taps of the farm bell. It hung in a great big tree. He read a paper from his side porch telling them they free. They been free several months then and didn't a one of them know it."*

This is a very special interview because I remember my Big Mama so well, and now I have a document of her explaining what life was like for her father, mother, grandmother, and other relatives during their time in slavery and after they were freed. Thank you, Ramon, for your research. This document is priceless!

# My Journey

**SPECIAL AUNTS AND UNCLES**

Having such a large extended family, it goes without saying I had a lot of aunts and uncles. But I will only briefly mention three who stand out in my mind as I reflect on my childhood.

David Smith, Sr.         Irene Smith *(a.k.a. Ma Fat)*

**DAVID AND IRENE SMITH**

First, let me mention Uncle David and Ma Fat, who lived directly across the street from us when I was a kid. Ma Fat was a very soft-spoken lady who was always so nice and kind to all of us kids. She was my mother's sister and they looked out for each other. I remember how she used to bake several large cakes for Christmas, and we looked forward to stopping by on Christmas Day to get some of the cake and candy. I don't ever remember Ma Fat fussing at me for anything.

# My Journey

Uncle David was the type of uncle who loved to tell jokes and BIG LIES, and he loved to talk about his army days. He would start telling one of his big lies and laugh louder than us kids. We loved being around Uncle David because he would take the time to talk to us young kids about anything we wanted to discuss. He used to tell me I had better stay in school and make something of myself because, in his words, *"Boy, you better go to school and study because you are going to be too little to do anything else!"* He used to joke about me being the smallest of the kids but that I was carrying more books than anyone else. Uncle David was a lot of fun!

Sometimes when David Jr. *(a.k.a. Hook)* would do something wrong, Uncle David would sit him down and chastise him before giving him a whipping. Most times, Hook would inch closer and closer to the door, and then just as Uncle David was getting ready to whip him, he would dash out the door and run as fast as he could. Uncle David would jump up and scream, "Go catch him!" But Hook was extremely fast, and we couldn't catch him. He would stay away for quite a while before returning home. Usually, by that time, Uncle David would have cooled down and decided not to whip him.

# My Journey

Clarence and Annie B. Williams
*(a.k.a. Uncle Clarence and Aunt Bee)*

## CLARENCE AND ANNIE BEE WILLIAMS

Uncle Clarence and Aunt Bee lived in St. Louis, Missouri, and would visit Brinkley nearly every summer to visit their extended family. Uncle Clarence was one of mama's big brothers, and she said he was very protective of her when she was little

We were always extremely happy when they visited Brinkley because it allowed us to spend time with their kids, *our*

# My Journey

*first cousins (Doris, Ree, Bud, Tommie, and Pat)*. Another reason was Uncle Clarence always gave each of us kids a "dime."

It was as if he had given us $100 each. His gesture of love and kindness never escaped me. Even to this day, I still remember and appreciate Uncle Clarence for caring so much for all the little kids in his family. We looked up to him! He was special.

Dorothy Williams
*(a.k.a. Aunt Dorothy)*

# My Journey

**DOROTHY WILLIAMS**

Aunt Dorothy was one of Mama's sisters who lived for a time in Chicago, St. Louis, and on the West End in Brinkley. There was one thing you could count on every day: Aunt Dorothy was going to drink some alcohol. When she lived in St. Louis, there was a liquor store a few steps from where she, Mama, and Uncle Clarence lived.

She would send one of the nieces or nephews to the store and tell them to ask the store owner, Jack, to send her a *"Dorothy Special!"* The store owner would know exactly what to send. Aunt Dorothy was a lot of fun. Sometimes she would get upset with some of the youngsters and cuss them out and everybody else would just laugh. Aunt Dorothy really loved all of us kids, and we loved her too. Aunt Dorothy is the one who nicknamed me "Pee Wee."

# My Journey

My Journey

## Chapter VI: Attending Public School

When I was in about the 4th or 5th grade, someone broke into our elementary school and took the money from the vault. A window hidden from the street was broken out on the side of the building. The burglar(s) then pried open the door to the principal's office. Once they got into the office, they knocked out a very large hole in the cinder block wall that was big enough for them to get through and then had full access to everything in the vault. They took the money from our fundraising drives. I don't remember anyone ever being arrested and charged for that crime.

# My Journey

I remember hearing all sorts of theories about who may have committed this offense, even the principal. Not sure who did this, but I remember it just as if it happened a year ago. Having spent most of my professional career as a school principal, I realize how frequently the principal gets lied on and blamed for seemingly everything that goes wrong. So, I do not believe for one minute that my principal had any involvement in this offense. I admired my principal, and his son was also my classmate and friend.

**My Elementary School Building for Grades K-6** *(Now torn down)*

**ELEMENTARY SCHOOL EXPERIENCES**

# My Journey

Prior to entering 1st grade, my mother would spend time trying to teach me different things like the alphabet, counting, etc. For reasons unknown to me, sometimes I would clam up and refuse to answer when she would ask me a question. I was very stubborn before I started school.

But one thing that stands out is even though I sometimes refused to cooperate with my mother, I WAS STILL LEARNING THE INFORMATION! By the time I entered 1st grade, I quickly began grasping the material because my mother had done a good job teaching me, even when I did not want to do my part.

*Lesson Learned: Parents, even if your child becomes a little stubborn at times, don't give up; keep teaching them just as my mother did with me, and it will manifest itself as time goes on.*

There were two activities I remember from my elementary school days that I really enjoyed participating in: Spelling Bees and School Plays.

## SPELLING BEES

The teacher would stand us up at the front of the room and go down the line giving each of us a word to spell. If you missed your word, you would have to sit down. This would continue until the last person stood and declared the WINNER! This was a lot of fun, and I usually did quite well because I was a pretty good speller in those days. I enjoyed the competition.

**SCHOOL PLAYS**

I was cast in most of the plays we had in our school. In one of our plays, I thought I was getting married to this little girl I liked so much *(of course I did not let her know it)*. To me, she was the prettiest girl in the whole school, and I thought I would be the one to marry her in the play. Man, I was so happy! Then I discovered I was not; instead, I was the "ring-bearer." To my dismay, another boy was chosen. I was SO naïve! I was also crushed!

**UFO SIGHTING**

When I was in about the 5th or 6th grade, I sincerely believe I saw a **UFO**. It was a warm, quiet night and I was asleep in my bed with my head lying against the window to get some air. We had a screen on the window. I did not hear anything, but something woke me up. At that moment, I looked up at the sky and saw an object that was not moving or making any sounds. That's why I knew it was not a helicopter. There were lights attached to this object. I honestly don't remember seeing it disappear.

# My Journey

I could remember everything I had seen when I woke up the next morning. So, when I got to school that day, I overheard my principal talking to another man about what he had seen the previous night. What he described is exactly what I had seen. I was afraid to say anything because I was so young, and these were adults talking. *We were taught children are not to get into adult conversations.* Besides, he was my principal! I wish I had spoken up because it would have validated what I believed I had seen and validated it for the principal. To this day, I still believe I saw **what I saw**!

**AFTERSCHOOL FIGHT**

Around the age of nine or ten, I got into a fight with two White boys. I was coming home from school, walking on the sidewalk, minding my business. These two White boys stepped out of their yard onto the sidewalk, blocked my path, and refused to let me pass. When I tried to force my way through them, they began to hit me, and the fight was on!

One was about my size and the other was taller and chubby. Lucky for me, my cousin, Fred Marshall, was walking a few feet behind me. When he saw what was happening, he quickly

# My Journey

ran up the little hill to the sidewalk, grabbed the chubby kid, put his head between his legs and started whaling away on him.

In the meantime, I was doing a pretty good job of kicking the other kid's butt. Then, their mother ran out of nowhere screaming and hollering at us. We immediately started running home as fast as we could. Their mother jumped in her car and followed us home.

She told a bunch of lies about how we had jumped on her children and beat them up. She screamed at my older relatives, threatened them and demanded something better be done. I remember my aunt apologizing to the woman and telling her we would get a whipping when our parents came home from work.

Well, Fred Marshall's folks did not whip him. But when my mama got home, my aunt and grandmother told her how angry and upset that White lady was and encouraged mama to whip me. I tried to explain to mama that those boys started the fight, and I was only protecting myself. She whipped me anyway.

After the whipping, I was devastated because I felt like mama had whipped me for defending myself! I have thought about this over the years. Now I realize mama, in her way, was protecting *her child* from danger. This happened in 1956 or 1957 in the segregated south, and most Black people feared Whites because of

## My Journey

all the lynchings and other violence perpetrated against Black people.

I think she was afraid of what those angry White people might try to do to me. After all, it was just a year or so earlier that Emmitt Till was brutally murdered in Mississippi for supposedly whistling at a White woman. Mama didn't want anything to happen to me. In her own way, she was trying to protect me from those angry, racist "White people."

**SHOOTING HOOKY (TRUANCY)**

When I was in 5th or 6$^{th}$ grade, my best friend, Eugene Harris, and I decided we would shoot hooky from school. *(For those who may not know, shooting hooky simply means you skip school or class without permission.)* I don't know whose idea this was, but we agreed to do it, thinking we would have a lot of fun playing while the other kids were in school. Two things we did not think through before shooting hooky: *boredom* setting in and *hunger*. Well, we experienced both before lunchtime. After all, two young boys can only play for so long before they get bored, not to mention having nothing to eat.

# My Journey

There was a field across the street from the school with tall weeds, and we ended up getting down really low and sneaking up as close to the street as we could without being seen.

It was lunchtime and all the kids were outside running, playing and having such a great time. We felt like fools laying there in the weeds while the other kids were on the playground enjoying themselves, WITH FULL STOMACHS! Well, we couldn't wait to return to school the next day, and we never tried that again.

**ELEMENTARY SCHOOL TEACHERS**

Let me introduce you to some of my elementary school teachers, starting with my favorite:

## Mrs. Bennie Randolph Bryant Adams
## My teacher in Grades 1-3

# My Journey

**Ms. Bryant at my home in Dallas in 1984**

Ms. Bryant, WOW! Where do I begin? If you look in the dictionary for the definition of a "Master Teacher," you should see Ms. Bryant's picture. Ms. Bryant took me under her wing and taught me in grades one, two, & three *(We didn't have kindergarten.)*. And as the story goes, when I was promoted to fourth grade, I showed up at Ms. Bryant's door again. That's when she said, *"Little Butler Boy, you have to go to your 4$^{th}$-grade teacher this year. I can't be your teacher until you finish college!"*

Ms. Bryant motivated me and helped lay the foundation for a lifelong love for learning and a successful career in education. We were also church members until I moved my family to Flint, Michigan, in 1970. Ms. Bryant was extremely kind, loving, and very supportive. But at the same time, she was very demanding and would not accept anything less than your best.

When I received my appointment as principal of W. W. Bushman Elementary School in 1984, Ms. Bryant traveled from California to visit me for a few days. I was ecstatic! She told me how proud she was of me! What a humbling experience for me. I was so honored to have this educational giant come and stay in my home with my family and me.

# My Journey

During our few days together, we spent countless hours talking about our love for teaching and the need for today's teachers to take the educational well-being of ALL children more seriously. As my wife watched and listened to us talk, she said she had finally met someone as passionate about children's education as her husband. Ms. Bryant and I kept in touch until she passed on January 3, 1996. Even to this day, I still think of Ms. Bryant, and she remains a major influence in my life!

**Ms. Bryant with me at W. W. Bushman Elementary School in August 1984 My 1st Principal Assignment.**

# My Journey

## Ms. Lula Ester Campbell – My 6th Grade Teacher

Ms. Campbell was my sixth-grade teacher. Two things come to mind that I remember from her class: 1) During one of our class assignments, Ms. Campbell had all the students write about our Philosophy of Education. I remember writing that I wanted to grow up, go to college and become a teacher to help others.

I stuck to this philosophy because I became a teacher. During my fifty years in education *(full-time & part-time)*, I assisted and inspired many students, teachers, parents, administrators, and hopefully, my own children and grandchildren.

Some of my former students are now medical doctors, attorneys, teachers, ministers, principals, college administrators, entrepreneurs, politicians, etc. 2) Ms. Campbell would always say to the girls: *"Pretty is as pretty does!"* This was her way of teaching the girls how to always conduct themselves as young ladies.

## Ms. I. W. Truesdale – My 5th Grade Teacher

Mrs. Truesdale was a very strict teacher who demanded excellence from her students. She had a way of positioning her eyeglasses so we little kids would think she was looking down at her book when she was really looking over the top of her glasses to catch us talking. I do remember her singling me out more than once for talking. She was a good teacher who wanted the best for us.

### Mrs. Novella Burton – 6th Grade Teacher

Ms. Burton was a no-nonsense teacher who was very strict and did not "spare the rod" when someone was acting out. I don't remember her being my teacher, but I remember getting a good whipping from her once. It was lunchtime and I was outside playing with my best friend, Eugene Harris. For some reason, we decided to pick up these little branches and started chasing the girls. We were only playing with them and were not planning to hit or hurt them.

As we chased the girls, they began screaming and hollering playfully. But this loud noise caught the attention of Ms. Burton, and she screamed at us from her window and demanded that Eugene and I come to her classroom and bring the switches with us.

After we got to her classroom, she asked us why we were chasing those girls. I quickly spoke up and lied by saying I was not chasing them. Eugene admitted we were just playing with them and were not going to hit them. At that point, Ms. Burton told him he could sit down because he had told the truth. She told me she would whip me because she was standing in the window watching both of us chase those girls. She complimented Eugene for telling the truth and then whipped me for lying. Man, that whipping really hurt! *Lesson Learned: Always tell the truth, even if it means you may get in trouble. Remember, sometimes it may even get you out of trouble.*

## HEALTH CHALLENGES IN ELEMENTARY SCHOOL

### POLIO SCARE

When I was about 7 or 8 years old, one of my legs stiffened up, and it drew up to the point where my foot heel nearly touched my buttock. I could not straighten it out. It was very scary. My parents took me to a doctor, and after he examined me, he told my parents that I had Polio. *(Polio is an infectious disease caused by a virus that can spread from person to person and causes paralysis. It was prevalent during that time.)*

Luckily, my father was a very shrewd man and did not accept the diagnosis from the first doctor. He immediately took me

# My Journey

to another doctor the same day for a second opinion. His name was Dr. Dalton. After his examination, Dr. Dalton told my parents I DID NOT have Polio.

He instructed them to take me home and apply hot towels *(as hot as I could bear) to my leg for about 30 minutes and that it* should straighten out. Thank God he was right! My leg did straighten out and I have never had that problem again. To this day, I don't remember what the doctor said caused the problem. *Lesson Learned: It pays to get a second opinion.*

**BB GUN INCIDENT**

When I was about 8 or 9 years old, my younger brother, Larry, shot me in my left eye with a BB gun. Ironically, we had been shooting and playing with that BB gun all day and thought there were NO BBs in the gun. Apparently, one had gotten hung up in the chamber. I was standing at the corner of one of our rooms and Larry was at the other corner with the BB gun.

As I peered out from the corner to see where Larry was, he pulled the trigger and a BB came out and hit me dead in my left eyeball. The pain was excruciating, and I ran around the house screaming and yelling at the top of my lungs. I remember my head

# My Journey

began pounding immediately. Because my parents were at work, I had to suffer until they got home that evening.

When they arrived, my brothers and I told them what had happened. They didn't think the BB had hit the inside of my eye, so they did not take me to the doctor. I laid around for a few days complaining about the severe pain I was experiencing from my eye, and my head was also pounding non-stop! Not to mention I was also unable to see out of that eye. Finally, after complaining for two or three days, they took me to the doctor.

When the doctor examined me, he could not believe what he saw. He told my parents the BB was still in my head. The BB had settled way up my temple, resting between my outer skin and my skull; you could see it protruding under the skin.

The doctor took his fingers, pushed, and guided the BB down until it came out of my eye. It hit the floor and rolled across the room. But by this time, the damage had already been done. He said the BB had caused an infection in my eye and I would most likely have poor vision in that eye.

The doctor recommended that I begin wearing eyeglasses. I never liked wearing eyeglasses because they did nothing to improve the vision in my eye, plus they were ugly. So, I broke them a couple of times and my parents gave up on the eyeglasses. *Yes!*

# My Journey

Later, I will discuss how the injury to my left eye negatively impacted me throughout my life *(limited vision and migraine headaches)*, especially when I began playing sports in junior and senior high school.

**Marian Anderson High School for Grades 7-12** *(Now torn down)*
(NOTE: My mother attended high school in this building, and so did I. My first teaching job was in this building.)

## HIGH SCHOOL EXPERIENCES

I remember being nervous and excited when I began 7$^{th}$ grade. Going from the elementary school building to the high school building was a "scary thing" to me. Right at the front of the

## My Journey

high school building was a set of steps. It was only about five or six steps, but they seemed so high at the time.

Just walking up those steps was bad enough, but when I entered the building, everything looked much bigger than what I had grown accustomed to in the elementary school building. When I left the sixth grade, I was bigger than most kids in the *lower* grades. Seeing all those BIG KIDS from grades 7-12 walking around took some getting used to. It was quite a shock!

Then to add to this fear, there were a lot of new kids in $7^{th}$ grade that I had never seen before. We had students bused in from smaller towns like Wheatley, Palestine, Goodwin, and other surrounding areas. They came to Brinkley because their towns were too small to have a high school.

After they finished grade six in their town, they would attend high school in Brinkley. Most were nice and respectable, but some came with attitudes and behavior problems.

I remember this one new kid in my class named J. C. Smith. His cousins called him Jeff. Anyway, J. C. loved to *play the dozens* and harass you throughout the day.

*(Our version of playing the dozens simply meant that we would talk about each other's mama in a playful way to generate a laugh from our friends.)*

# My Journey

So, I started playing the *dozens* with him to see who could get the best of each other.

He learned my mother's name was Catherine (she later began spelling it like this: Cathryn.) J. C. loved to get me riled up, "*Casterine*, she's my queen!" He wouldn't say Catherine. I don't remember us ever taking it to the point of becoming angry with each other. It was all good fun.

**THE BULLY**

Another boy began attending our school in the 7th grade and he came with a mean spirit and was always arguing and harassing other students. He was the classic definition of a bully. I will not use his real name in this book, so I will call him Josh. When he spoke, he had a growl and a harsh tone, which alone scared most of us. Finally, one day in our physical education class, he got in the face of the wrong boy. That boy was Calvin Hill.

Now, Calvin never picked on anyone and was very friendly and liked to joke around. But when Josh got in Calvin's face and pushed him, oh my goodness, Calvin commenced lighting him up! I mean, Calvin was all over him. When the fight was finally stopped, Josh was bleeding profusely from his nose and mouth.

# My Journey

All I could think was, YES! Finally, someone had the courage to stand up to this bully. Calvin became my hero that day. We remained friends throughout high school and college, and to this day, we are still friends. By the way, I don't remember Josh bothering anyone else after taking that beating from Calvin!

**BOY SCOUTS**

I was a member of the Boy Scouts of America in the $6^{th}$ and $7^{th}$ grades. I think I dropped out of scouting because my family could not afford to purchase me a scout uniform. I felt sort of "left out," so I eventually quit. But, while I was a scout, I enjoyed the activities and learning the scout's Oath, Motto, and Slogan, which we recited at each scout meeting.

I remember sometimes the scoutmasters would lace us up with boxing gloves and then pair us off to box. I got my first "knockdown" in one of those matches. They paired me off with this kid I thought could beat me because he talked a good game and ran his mouth all the time. I don't know how I did it, but I got lucky and landed the right punch at the right time, and down he went. Man, you couldn't tell me anything after that happened. I thought I had really done something special.

# My Journey

**THURSDAY NIGHT SOCIALS**

Our high school allowed us to have school-sponsored socials on Thursday nights. I'm not sure, but I think this happened twice a month. It was an opportunity for us to socialize and interact with each other while dancing and having a great time. It was also a small fundraiser for the school.

I remember one Thursday night when Bobby, Acy, and I had gotten dressed for the social. Daddy stopped us at the door and asked us where we were going. After telling him that we were going to the school social, he said we could not go and instructed us to go back to our room. Now, Bobby was 16, Acy was almost 15, and I was 12 or 13.

After we got back into our bedroom, Bobby asked us what we would do. Hey, I was only twelve or thirteen, so I knew exactly what I would do: STAY HOME! And that's exactly what I told them I was going to do. Acy said he wasn't sure yet. That's when Bobby spoke up and said, "I'm going!" He then proceeded to walk right out the front door without hesitation.

All I could think was, Oh Crap! No, he didn't. In the meantime, Acy thought he could out-smart daddy. So, he fashioned some clothes in his bed in the shape of a person and pulled the

# My Journey

cover over it, hoping daddy would think he was in bed if he came to our room to check on us.

As Bobby slammed the front door, daddy ran to the door and asked who had gone out the door. When he learned it was Bobby, he called out to him, but Bobby never broke his stride. With each step, you could hear the rocks crunching under the weight of his feet as he made his way up that rocky road. Daddy continued to scream out his name, but Bobby never answered him.

Daddy was furious and stormed into our room to see if we were there. Boy, when he looked in Acy's bed and found those clothes under the cover, he was livid and began ranting and raving about how he would beat them when they got home.

He sat in a chair by the door waiting for them to get home. Well, Acy didn't know he was busted, so he climbed back in through the same window, thinking he had gotten away with his little stunt. Bobby, however, walked right back through the front door like the YOUNG MAN he had become.

Daddy immediately grabbed him and began trying to whip him with a belt. It should be noted Bobby had apparently already made up his mind that he would NOT take any more whippings from daddy. As daddy tried to whip him, Bobby grabbed the belt, took it from daddy, and threw it to the floor.

# My Journey

He then raised his fists, took a combative stance, and said to daddy, "I'm not taking any more whippings! If you want to whip me, you're going to have to whip me with these!" Daddy looked at him, thought for a second, then just walked away.

As a young kid, I could not believe what I had just witnessed. My big brother, Bobby, had just stood his ground with CHARLIE BUTLER and declared himself a MAN! But daddy wasn't finished. Remember, he had found the clothes in Acy's bed, so he quickly came to our bedroom, pulled Acy out, and commenced whipping him. I think he was taking some of his anger from his confrontation with Bobby out on Acy.

Me, I was just glad I had enough sense to keep my little butt at home. The next day, daddy told mama and some of our older relatives he realized Bobby had become too big to try to whip and he would not attempt to whip him anymore.

Without a doubt, daddy knew Bobby could take care of himself when it came to "doing battle." You see, not only did my big brother box on our school's boxing team *(with gloves),* but he also regularly boxed different guys around town, and they boxed with **bare knuckles!**

# My Journey

He was tough as nails, but he never was a bully or picked on anyone. He was the total opposite and never bragged about his boxing skills. He was just a good person.

**Bobby was 18 when this picture was taken.**

**Bobby Butler, you're a Bad Man! (MY BIG BROTHER)**

**FIRST CAR**

When I was a junior in high school and Acy was a senior, daddy bought us our first car. The car was a dark green 1954 DeSoto and it was in bad shape. I remember the person he bought it from had driven it from Chicago and decided it was not in good enough condition to make it back to Chicago. So, he sold it to daddy for $35, just enough to purchase a bus ticket to Chicago.

# My Journey

Man, we were excited when we first got the car. But we quickly realized it had many, many problems.

One of the first things we noticed was when the car was going down the street; it was sort of going sideways. I think the frame of the car had been bent in an accident causing it to travel down the street in that manner. The next thing was we never knew when it might decide NOT to start.

There were times when we would drive it to school and at the end of the day, we would quickly get to the car to see if it would start before a lot of people came outside. Oftentimes, it would not start. On those days, we would stand outside the car or sit in it trying to *'style and profile.'* We tried to look cool and not let on to anyone that our car wouldn't start.

After almost everyone had left the campus, we would try to push the car to get it to start. Sometimes it worked; sometimes, it didn't. We certainly did not have the money to complete the repairs, so we eventually got rid of it because it was embarrassing to let our classmates see us pushing our car to try to start it.

# My Journey

**Lincoln Butler, Fred Marshall, Calvin Hill – 12th Grade**

*We took this picture while getting ready to leave for Washington, D.C., for our Senior Class Trip, in May 1965. We were **"reenacting"** our pose when the police told us to get out of the car with our hands up! (Read on.)*

## TAKEN INTO POLICE CUSTODY

It was a Saturday night, and all the teenagers and young adults were "hanging out" around the little night spots across the tracks in Brinkley. The three of us (Fred Marshall, Calvin Hill, and me) were sitting in my cousin Mackie's car. We were all seniors in high school. I was sitting in the driver's seat, Fred was in the front passenger seat, and Calvin was in the back seat. Leamon Briggs, Cousin Mackie's grandson, had driven the car that night and was inside the pool hall.

Out of nowhere, Leamon's older half-brother opened the door on the driver's side and told me to slide over. I don't remember his name, so I will refer to him as Jason. Jason had gotten the keys from Leamon and told us he had a little run to make.

# My Journey

We were getting ready to get out of the car when he told us we could stay because he would be returning. He indicated he was just going up the street to cash his check.

When Jason got to the store, we all stayed in the car. He went into the store but quickly came back out. He didn't say anything, but we noticed he did not turn the car lights on when he left the store. After a few blocks, the police got behind us with their lights flashing. That's when Jason told us he tried to cash a bad check. Instead of pulling over and stopping the car, he began to accelerate faster and faster. The police were right upon us.

Without a doubt, we were afraid and begged Jason to stop the car, but he continued to speed up. This was in 1965 and he was headed toward the interstate highway that was being constructed on the north end of town. There was a lot of construction with many barricades and curves to navigate around. Jason was driving extremely fast, and the police were right behind us. Jason started hitting some of the wood barricades and objects started flying all over the place.

About that time, Fred screamed for us to get down, so the three of us got down as low as we could. Seemingly, at that very moment, a large piece of wood from one of those barricades came straight through the middle of the windshield where my head

# My Journey

would have been if Fred hadn't told us to get down. Only God knows what may have happened if I had not gotten down. That large piece of wood lodged through the glass about two or three feet inside the car. Glory Be to God none of us got injured!

Jason then lost control of the car, went down a ditch and through a wire fence, and ended up in a field. Immediately after the car came to a stop, the police ran up *(with their guns ready)* and screamed at us to get out with our hands up. We were very frightened because we didn't know if they were going to shoot us or not.

They took all of us down to the police station and quickly took Jason to a cell. They questioned the three of us and gave us a date to come back to appear in court before a judge. They then released us to go home. I don't think I had ever been so afraid. When we appeared for our court date, we were told Jason had confessed to everything and told them we had nothing to do with any of it. We were not charged with anything and did not have to appear in court. They allowed us to go back to school. Thank God.

**PROM DATE**

When I was in the 12th grade, I asked my social studies teacher, Ms. Wilson, if she would go to the prom with me. To my surprise, she said yes! Now, you know I was only joking with her, so naturally, I did not attempt to follow through with this and never made any attempts to contact her. Honestly, I was already making big plans to take my girlfriend to the prom. Well, as you might expect, Ms. Wilson gave me a hard time that next week when we returned to school.

She told the class I had asked her to go to the prom with me and then stood her up. She told them she had gotten dressed and was waiting for me to pick her up. Everyone laughed and made fun of me for standing the teacher up. They really gave me a hard time. Of course, she was just kidding and wanted to see my reaction. This was all done in good fun! Ms. Wilson was one of those teachers who really knew how to connect with her students. I enjoyed her class.

**SCHOOL PLAYS**

While in high school, I participated in different school activities. I sang in the school choir and was cast in a couple of exciting school plays. While in the 11$^{th}$ grade, I starred in a "Pigmeat Markham" production. He was a comedian whose jokes were funny but sometimes a bit raunchy. I guess I did a pretty good job in that role because I was cast as the lead actor in my Senior

## My Journey

Class Play the next year and consequently won the "Best Actor" award.

The title of the senior class play was "Grandpa's Twin Sister." As the name suggests, I played two characters in that play: I was Grandpa Hatcher *(A cantankerous old man),* and I also played his twin sister. This was an awesome play, and I had a great time starring in the lead role! I still remember my opening lines:

*"Betty! Maggie! Louise!"; "Betty! Maggie! Louise!"; "Confound it, where's my medicine?"*

**FOR THE LOVE OF BASKETBALL**

I always liked sports, especially basketball, and therefore spent a lot of time practicing and playing. I made the basketball team in junior and senior high school. We had some outstanding athletes in our school, and as a result, I was not a starter, but I did get to play occasionally.

There weren't many things for Black kids to do growing up poor in a small town. Therefore, my brothers, cousins, and I played a lot of basketball and baseball. I remember we used to do something that would have gotten us into a lot of trouble at home and at school if we had gotten caught. We would **sneak** into the gym on Sunday evenings and play basketball. *(My wife said we were criminals and should have been charged with B&E.)*

# My Journey

Anyway, this is how we did it. At the end of the day, on Fridays, someone would make sure a window was left unlocked in the gym so we could get back in on Sunday. At first, we could get in through one of the coach's windows, and then that person would just let the rest of us in through the gym's back door. There were NO alarms on the doors.

I guess the coach started double-checking his windows before leaving on Friday because all his windows would be locked when we tried to enter. So, we would walk around the gym until we saw a partially open window. We would then lift someone very athletic up over our heads so they could reach the window ledge and then pull themselves up, climb through the window, and drop to the floor. That person was usually David, Jr. (Hook) because he was indeed the most athletic. He would then let the rest of us in through the back door.

We would have a great time, which also helped improve our game. We never caused any damage and always left the gym clean as we found it. Luckily for us, we never got caught.

***FEARLESS OR INSANE?***

In addition to playing basketball, I was also on the football team. Our high school did not get a football team or band program until my senior year. I honestly did not know much about football in terms of the responsibilities of each position. During our after-school practices, I was always used as a running back.

When I finally got to play in one of our games, the coach put me in as a defensive end and told me which guy to defend. Man, that dude went blazing down the sideline and when I realized what was happening, I was in pursuit of him, about 10 yards behind. The ball was thrown in his direction, but luckily for me, it was overthrown, and the play came back. The coach quickly called me to the sideline and benched me!

Shortly afterward, the weather got cold and that's when I realized football was not for me. So, I quit the team. Hey, it got cold out there *"riding that bench"* game after game. I decided it made more sense to sit in a warm car watching the game with my girlfriend than sliding up and down that cold bench.

**WORKING AS A MAID**

While I was in high school, I worked as a maid in the home of our school superintendent, Mr. Partee. His wife, Mrs. Partee, hired me to do her domestic work. My brother Bobby held this job for his last year in high school, and after graduating, I asked Mrs. Partee if I could have the job. Some chores included washing dishes, washing clothes, and hanging them outside on the clotheslines, ironing, making beds, sweeping the porch and the sidewalks, etc.

I worked every Saturday morning from 9:00 – 12 noon and was paid one dollar per hour. This little job came in handy because I had money in my pocket for the next week. I held on to this job throughout my junior and senior years of high school.

## HEALTH CHALLENGES IN HIGH SCHOOL

**Effects of Eye Injury**

I mentioned earlier how I suffered an injury to my left eye. I want to share how this injury and other health issues affected me in high school. First, playing sports became somewhat risky and even dangerous because of the limited vision on my left side. By the way, I never let ANYONE outside of my immediate family know the severity of the injury to my left eye. It was too embarrassing. Let me give you some examples of how it impacted my life:

**Boxing**

As a kid, whenever I boxed with someone, I often got hit on

# My Journey

my left side, and I now know why. I could not see the punch coming until it was about to land upside my head! I was just a kid, so I did not associate that with the eye injury at the time.

**Basketball**

I frequently got called for fouls because if someone came up from behind me and set a screen or "pick" on my left side, I would often run into them as I quickly turned to go left, trying to defend the person with the ball.

**Baseball**

I loved baseball, but I was poor at batting and now I know why. I am right-handed so the ball is always coming at me from my left side. By the time I picked the ball up in my vision field, it was already passing me. Thus, I would swing late. I can still hear the coach screaming, *"Butler, you're swinging too late!"* He didn't know about my eye injury.

**Driving**

I have always had to be extremely careful when driving because it is hard to see cars coming up on me from my left side. I must constantly check and double-check my rearview and side mirrors, especially when getting ready to switch to a left lane. In addition to checking my mirrors, I always turn and look over my left shoulder before changing lanes to my left.

**Sitting In Meetings**

I hate when I'm sitting in a meeting and the hand-outs come from my left. If I am not aware that the document is coming my way, the person seated next to me will have to pass it all the way in front of me, or they will nudge me in some way to get my attention. This is, to say the least, embarrassing! So, when I know that hand-outs are coming from the left side, I try to angle myself slightly to the left so I can see when the person is passing them to me.

**Military Classification**

From 1940-1973, young men had to register for the military draft when they turned eighteen. I remember leaving college for a couple of days in 1965 to go to Little Rock to take a physical and a battery of tests. After completing my registration and physical, I received my classification notice sometime later. Now, the Selective Service will issue you a classification based on your test results. The following are some of the classifications one could receive: 1-A (eligible for military service); 3-A – (Hardship

# My Journey

Deferment); 2-S – Student deferment because of enrollment as a college student; 4-F – (Disabled and Unfit for Military Service).

Because of the *injury to my left eye*, I received the 4-F Classification (later changed to 1-Y) – "Disabled and Unfit for Military Service." Even though I did not want to go into the military because the Vietnam War was in full force at the time, I was still extremely embarrassed to have a 4-F Classification.

Who wants to be labeled as **unfit**? I didn't want anyone to know my real classification, so I told everyone that I had gotten the 2-S student deferment classification because I was in college. *This is the reason why I did not serve in the military and most of my brothers did!*

**Lost Job Opportunity**

I remember in 1970, I applied for an administrative job at General Motors Corporation in Flint, Michigan. I think I did well in the interview, but when they conducted the vision test, I failed because of the injury to my left eye. I was told because of all the machinery and heavy equipment used in a big automotive factory, you must have good vision in both eyes, or one could easily get hurt, and that was a risk they could not take. Consequently, I did not get the job.

# My Journey

**Severe Migraine Headaches**

I have had to deal with severe migraine headaches throughout my life. I used to say there were two things I could count on in life: going to bed at night with a headache and waking up the next morning with a headache. These headaches started after I was shot in my left eye with the BB gun. In high school, I usually had a headache almost every day. At the end of the school day, we had to go "dress out" for football or basketball practice. In football, this was not easy because, in addition to dealing with the pounding headaches, there was also the heat from the blazing hot summer sun.

When I was in college, sometimes I would walk the floor all night, squeezing a pillow against my temples, trying to get even a second or two of relief from the pounding in my head. I would then have to be in class at 8:00 am like all the other students who probably got a good night's sleep. But even so, God still saw me through it all and brought me out safely on the other side. I made it, and I graduated with my class! I did not let anyone know about my headaches.

*Lesson Learned: Careless behavior during childhood can negatively impact the rest of your life! Be Careful.*

# My Journey

When faced with difficult challenges in life, I recommend reciting this quote from Dr. Robert Schuller:

**"Tough Times Never Last, But Tough People Do!"**

Despite the eye injury and the headaches, I was determined to succeed.

REMEMBER: NEVER GIVE UP!
Read the Poem: **"Don't Quit"**
by Edgar A. Guest

**MY BIGGEST REGRET IN HIGH SCHOOL**

I sincerely wish I had spent more time studying and preparing myself academically instead of wasting so much time and energy "chasing girls, playing basketball, and shooting pool."

Remember this quote from Brother Malcolm X: *"Education is our passport to the future. For tomorrow belongs only to those who prepare for it today."*

# My Journey

## MY HIGH SCHOOL DAYS ARE OVER!

### DADDY STAYED TRUE TO WHO HE WAS

I remember the evening after my high school graduation, I was still on a "natural high" after completing this milestone in my life. After all, you only graduate from high school once! So, I was still celebrating when daddy came home from work. I don't know what his problem was, but he started in on me about cutting the yard. I remember thinking how heartless he was for not understanding how elated I felt about my graduation. Come on now, couldn't the yard at least wait until tomorrow? I was so angry at him because of the way he tore into me, and I knew I was in for a long, miserable summer if I stayed home with him.

### FLINT, MICHIGAN, HERE I COME!

After finishing the yard work, I found Aunt Bird, who had come from Flint, Michigan, to attend the graduation in support of Fred Marshall, my cousin Lillie, and me. Aunt Bird is really my first cousin, but we always called her Aunt Bird because she was the same age as my mother, and she was always so nice to all of us. Anyway, after I found Aunt Bird, I asked her if I could go back

## My Journey

to Flint with her and work until college began in the fall. SHE SAID YES! I was so happy. She then said we had to go talk to my mother and get her approval, and of course, mama said yes.

So, I immediately started packing the few clothes I owned and waited with anticipation for the day to come when I would be safely tucked away in Aunt Bird's Buick convertible headed to Flint, Michigan. I was about as happy as I had ever been in my entire life. I was finally getting away from Charlie Butler! I felt like Aunt Bird was my savior. She had come and rescued me from the clutches of my father. Hallelujah!!!

**Ms. Willis Mae Fox** *(a.k.a. Aunt Bird)*

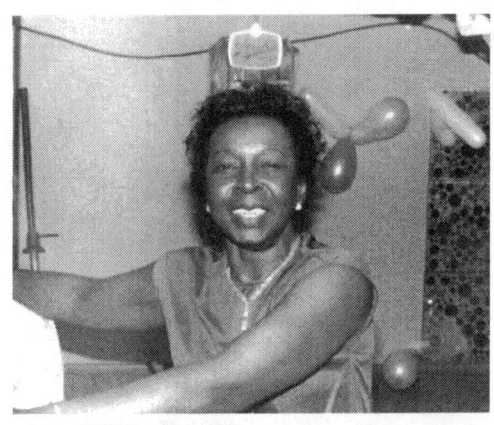

# My Journey

**Ms. Willis Mae Fox** *(a.k.a. Aunt Bird)*

*Me in Flint, MI (1965) and that's the Buick convertible at my back. Aunt Bird allowed me to drive her cars whenever I wanted to go out. I was so happy and grateful to be in Flint!*

Before I left Arkansas, I went to the college (AM&N) and took the entrance exam and another test to qualify for a "student

# My Journey

loan." My family did not have the money to send me to college, so I needed to pass that test to get a student loan. Quite honestly, I did not think I had passed the test. I had hung out with my friends most of the night before the test and had to get up early the next morning and ride 80 miles to the college where the test was administered. Since I was not feeling too good about the test, I told mama I was making plans to stay in Flint and go to Mott Jr. College.

  Then, a few days later, I received a call from mama, and boy, was she excited. As soon as I said hello, she screamed, "Lincoln, you passed the test for the student loan! You're going to college!" I truly don't know who was the most excited, me or my mama. As I think back to that time in my life, I thank God I passed that test because if I had failed it, I would have stayed in Flint and never met my beautiful wife.

# My Journey

# My Journey

## Chapter VII: Off To College

After being back in Brinkley for a few days, it was time to report to the college. My father drove me *(along with two of my high school friends, Benny Sneed & Herman Wells)* to Pine Bluff, Arkansas, to begin my college education. I remember experiencing excitement and nervousness as we turned off Cedar Street *(the main highway)* and entered the college grounds. Herman and Benny were my roommates during our first year of college.

Since elementary school, I dreamed of going to college and becoming a teacher. As a young student, teachers seemed to be the community's pillars and our role models. My two older brothers had gone off to the army, so I was the first in my family to attend college. Graduating from college was not an option for me because it was the only path I knew would allow me to provide a good life for my future wife and children. *(My older brothers joined me on campus after they finished their time in the army.)*

### THE DAY I MET THE LOVE OF MY LIFE

It was the first day of class registration, August 1965. I was in one of the lines with some homeboys inching my way toward the registration desk. Then, I turned to my right and looked at the people in another line registering for their classes. My heart began racing like it would jump out of my chest.

You see, I had just locked eyes with the most BEAUTIFUL WOMAN I had ever seen in my life! As I continued to inch forward, I would occasionally look back over at her, and sometimes she would stare back at me. No words were spoken. I then nudged my homeboys and declared to them that **I was looking at the woman I was going to marry!**

### DO YOU BELIEVE IN LOVE AT FIRST SIGHT? WELL, I DO!

# My Journey

**After stepping foot on Campus and unexpectantly seeing the woman of my dreams**

I had not spoken a word to her, so obviously I did not know her name. But I was convinced she was going to be my wife. *Now, I just had to find a way to convince her that I was going to be her husband.* Before I knew it, she was gone. I am thinking, who is she; where did she go? I must find her. I fell in love with this woman right then and there. Truly, this was love at first sight!

After completing my registration for that class, I was off to different location to register for another class. While standing in the second line, for whatever reason, I turned around and nearly fainted. There she was, the most beautiful woman I had ever seen

## My Journey

standing in line right behind me. And I mean right behind me; there was no one in between us. There I was, standing right next to MY FUTURE WIFE, but I didn't even know her name. I was in "awe" of her beauty!

At that moment, I struck up a "corny" conversation because I truly did not know what to say. I was so nervous now that I had her next to me. We acknowledged that we had noticed each other from the previous lines. We talked about where we were from and what we had done during the summer. She was from Tuscaloosa, Alabama, and had spent the summer in New York with her mother and other family members. I told her that I was from Brinkley, Arkansas, and had spent the summer in Flint, Michigan, with relatives.

Remember, this was the first day of class registration and I was afraid to ask her any personal questions, so I let her get away from me that day without getting any "follow-up" information on how to contact her later. Duh! I felt miserable afterward because it seemed like every time I saw her around the campus, she was usually with her male friend. All I was thinking was that is MY WIFE he was with, and I had to find a way to get her away from him.

# My Journey

At the beginning of the second semester (January 1966), there was a dance on campus, and I decided I was not going because I did not have a date. As fate would have it, Snow was at the dance, saw my homeboys, and asked about me.

They informed her I was not coming to the dance. She asked them to go tell me she wanted me to come to the dance. Man, I was so excited. My future wife wanted to see ME and had sent someone to get me. But you will not believe what happened next.

When I got to the dance, she was sitting next to her boyfriend! Once again, I was completely crushed. I felt like I had been punked! I am thinking, why the hell would she humiliate me like that? She knew she was there with her boyfriend, so why send for me and embarrass me like that?

I waited for a slow song to play so I could get close enough to her to ask why she had sent for me. Each time a slow song played, I approached her for a dance, but her boyfriend would grab her hand and lead her to the dance floor. He knew I was trying to get a dance with her so that was his way of keeping her away from me.

**MY HOMEBOY, CLARENCE TEAGUE**

# My Journey

Clarence was a year ahead of us in school, and he was a very outgoing individual. He related well to people and was very wise. So, I went around to the other side of the dance floor and told Clarence what was happening, and I let him know how badly I wanted to get the chance to talk to Snow. His plan was to stand behind them without them knowing it, and when a slow song came on, he instructed me to just make sure I reached for her hand before her boyfriend did. He then said for me not to worry because everything should be okay.

So, we waited for the slow song, and I immediately reached around Snow and asked her for a dance, and then her boyfriend asked her to dance. Snow spoke up and said to her boyfriend, *"He asked me first!"* She then proceeded to get up and dance with me. I escorted her deep into the crowded dance floor so I could talk to her. The length of the songs during that time was only about 2½ minutes, so I knew I only had a brief time to tell her all the things I had been waiting to say to her all semester. By the time the song finished, she had given me her dorm information and told me I could come and see her the next day. Hallelujah! It took nearly five months, but I had finally made real contact. Thank you, Clarence, for your wise counsel!

# My Journey

Oh yes, I was there the next day RIGHT ON TIME. We walked around the campus getting to know each other and quickly realized we had so much in common. We both came from large, low-income families. We had beautiful mothers whom we felt were angels. We both had *difficult* fathers, and that's putting it nicely. We both wanted more out of life than we had growing up. We both wanted children and wanted to put ourselves in a position to properly care for them. We both loved our families and wanted to grow up and help our mothers. We compared our siblings and found they were very similar as well. We had a wonderful time and really connected on our first *"getting to know you"* date.

**LET THE COURTSHIP BEGIN** *(All Eleven Months)*

Early on in our courtship, I asked Snow her birthdate. She told me she was born on May 21, 1947. Well, I was not born until September 12, 1947, which means she was a few months older than me. Because I was afraid she might stop dating me if she knew she was older, I told her my birthday was February 12, 1947. Hey, I was not going to risk taking a chance on losing this beautiful angel due to such a minor technicality as age. Over the next couple of months or so, we spent much time together and did not want to be away from each other. I always felt so special when walking

# My Journey

around the campus with Snow. It also did not hurt that she was absolutely one of the prettiest girls on campus!

One night when we were out on a date, I propositioned her in the wrong way, and buddy, she showed me some real ATTITUDE! She looked me straight in the eyes and said, "Who do you think you are? You can take me back to my dorm!" Man, she got my attention in a hurry. And yes, I immediately escorted her back to her dorm. *To be accurate, she was walking about five steps ahead of me*, and with every step, I was apologizing and asking for forgiveness. She was FUMING! When we got to her dorm, I asked her for a kiss and she said, **"Not in this lifetime!"**

Although I had "messed up" badly, I went to her dorm and called for her the next day. She came down without knowing it was me. I was standing there when she rounded the corner to enter the lobby. When she saw it was me, she started to walk off and I quickly grabbed her arm and begged her to talk to me. I apologized and asked her to please forgive me. I asked her if we could start over. She was still angry with me but did talk to me, and we eventually worked things out. She said it was not so much what I said but how I said it. *Lesson Learned: Take your time, and always be a gentleman!*

# My Journey

We continued to see each other regularly and became inseparable. I was so in love with this beautiful woman and nothing else mattered more than having her by my side. When spring break rolled around in April of 1966, we had been dating for almost four months. She was preparing to go home to Tuscaloosa, Alabama, and I was leaving for my hometown in Brinkley, Arkansas.

We rode the Greyhound bus together from our college in Pine Bluff to Brinkley. That is where I got off *without trying to get a kiss*. I wanted so badly to kiss her, but honestly, I was too nervous about attempting to kiss her on a bus filled with college kids. I was unsure how she would react, so I just said goodbye and got off the bus. I have always regretted not kissing her before leaving the bus.

After spring break, we returned to the campus and continued our courtship. When the semester ended, Snow went back to New York City, and I went back to Flint, Michigan. We stayed in touch through letters and Sunday evening phone calls. *(We still have every letter we ever wrote to each other!)* That seemed like the longest summer ever. Being away from Snow that summer was one of the hardest things I have ever had to do. I was MISERABLE! Finally, the summer was ending, and it was time to head back to college and back into the presence of my sweet angel.

# My Journey

Then the phone rang. It was Snow! She sounded sad, and then she told me she would not return to college that semester because her brother was also getting ready to start college and her mom could only afford to send one of them. I was devastated! The woman of my dreams and the love of my life was not coming back to me. Did I mention I was DEVASTATED?

My homeboy, Phillip Jones, was the head counselor for Lewis Hall, the dormitory where I stayed. At the end of my freshman year, he gave me a job as a residence hall counselor starting my sophomore year. I was extremely happy and blessed to be able to participate in the "student work-study program," which helped finance my education. Therefore, I had to report back to the college about a week or so ahead of the other students. During this time, I felt like I was going crazy because I missed Snow so much and I did not want to be on campus without her.

One day another one of my homeboys, Howard Smith, came to my room to give me a message. As usual, I was playing cards (gambling) and dismissed him when he walked in. Howard was a minister and sometimes I did not want to hear his long sermons. So, he immediately became angry and turned to leave, adding, "I came here to give you a message from that little Hearns girl, but now I'm not telling you anything." I quickly jumped up and begged him to give me the message. You see, something happened, and Snow *was* able to come back to college.

I was so happy and nervous at the same time because the last thing she told me before I left Michigan was she would not be back. I finally got Howard to tell me what she said, and he convinced me she was, indeed, back on campus. I left my dorm and started down the sidewalk, headed toward the student union building where she had told Howard she would be.

To my amazement, there she was, the most beautiful woman I had ever seen was back on campus **and looking for me!** She was just standing in front of the student union building, looking toward my dorm, and that is when we made eye contact. At that moment, we both ran toward each other and embraced and held on to each other for a very long time. We were so happy to be in each other's arms again. Now, fifty-six years later, we are still happy to be holding on to each other! Thank you, Jesus, for giving me this precious angel. We were just teenagers, but we knew we were meant to be together for life.

**COLLEGE LIFE**

When I was not on a date *(walking around campus)* with Snow; working my shift in the dormitory; working my shift in the

# My Journey

archaeology department; in class; or studying; I was usually playing cards *(gambling)*. I was rather good, but sometimes I cheated. One of my friends from high school also liked playing cards for money. It should be noted that his family had MONEY. They would send him a "blank check," and he would fill in the amount he wanted or needed. Well, this certainly worked in my favor because I was quite *crafty* when handling the cards and my friend was an easy target.

As time passed, I used to wait for him to cash his check so I could get him into a card game and win some of his money. Eventually, I became careless with my shenanigans, and one day while we were playing cards, I took too long to switch out my high cards for the aces I had hidden and that's when he stood up quickly and saw what I was doing. He became "unglued!"

He said, *"Lincoln Butler, you've been cheating me out of my money all along! I am going to kill you!"* He dove across the table and we began tussling. After a while, we fell into the window and I retrieved a screwdriver that we kept there. In one motion, I shoved him backward with one hand, raised the screwdriver with the other in a threatening manner, and forced him out of my room. I was NOT going to hurt him. I just had to get him off me. We remained good friends and are still friends to this day.

# My Journey

**BACK TO SNOW**

Snow and I continued to spend a lot of time together and around October or early November of 1966, I took her to the doctor, and he told us she was pregnant. I knew we loved each other, and I was NOT about to abandon her. So, we decided we wanted to be together for the rest of our lives. *(We later realized that the so-called pregnancy was a false alarm.)* But that really did not matter because we did not want to be apart.

**WE WERE ONLY 19 YEARS OLD, BUT WHEN YOU KNOW, YOU KNOW.**

After Snow and I completed the paperwork for our marriage license and took our blood test, there was still one minor problem: I needed one of my parents to sign the papers and get them notarized. In Arkansas, a male had to be twenty-one to get married without his parent's permission and I was only nineteen. Therefore, I had to ride the bus back home to Brinkley and get daddy to go to a notary with me and sign the marriage permit. Initially, he balked a little at the idea and was already in bed.

I told him I had never asked him for anything, and all I needed was for him to get up and go with me to get those papers notarized. I assured him would never ask him for anything else again. He eventually got out of bed and drove me to the notary to

## My Journey

sign the papers. I did not go back to the house with him. Instead, I waited "uptown" for the next bus back to my college campus.

Snow, my mom, and I then made plans for our wedding. Strangely enough, instead of getting married in our church, I wanted to get married in the house where I grew up. Mama tried to convince me the house was too small, but I persisted, and we did get married in my home.

**OUR WEDDING DAY**

Snow and I got married on Dec. 18, 1966. That day, she made me the happiest man in the world! Unfortunately, no members of her immediate family attended the wedding because they all lived in New York and were not financially able to make the trip. However, her mom and sister purchased her a beautiful wedding dress and sent it to her. *(Note: Years later, we renewed our vows in Tuscaloosa, AL, and most of her family were able to attend. It was a beautiful affair!)*

After we had recited our vows and were pronounced husband and wife, I remember sitting on the couch staring so lovingly into each other's eyes when my father walked up. I was not prepared for what came next. He looked at me and sarcastically said, *"Son, you're sitting there looking at her like you could eat*

## My Journey

*her up. In a year's time, you're going to wish you had!"* My God, what encouragement from your father right after you pledged before God your desire to love and honor this woman for the rest of your life. Each time I saw my father after that, I reminded him of the number of years we had been married up to that point, and I would proudly proclaim to him how much we still loved each other!

Clarence Teague, Linc & Snow, Rev. Johnson, Ella Bryant, Acy Butler *(Best Man)*

# My Journey

**Linc and Snow Cutting the Cake.**

After our wedding, we went to Snow's hometown, Tuscaloosa, Alabama, for our honeymoon. Her father was the only one in her immediate family still living there. I was a little nervous about meeting him because Snow's homeboys back on campus had been giving me a hard time about how her father may be upset with me because he did not like for anyone to "mess over his daughters." I remember telling them that I was not messing over his daughter because I loved her and was going to marry her! When we got to Tuscaloosa, her father was the opposite. He was very friendly toward me and took me around the entire neighborhood introducing me as his new son-in-law. In private, he asked me to take good care of her.

# My Journey

## FACING NEW CHALLENGES AND OBSTACLES

Shortly after our wedding, Snow became ill and could not attend school for the second semester. She returned to New York to stay with her mom that semester. Boy, I quickly learned what being lonely and heartbroken felt like. I never dreamed I could love someone so deeply and miss them so much. It felt like my whole world had ended when Snow got on that bus and headed back to Tuscaloosa, and from there, she rode a train to New York.

Back at college, my homeboys used to tease me a lot because I would mostly stay in my dorm room and lament over how much I missed my wife and worried about her health. They would say to each other, do not go around Lincoln Butler because the only thing he's going to do is stare at his wife's picture and talk about how much he misses her.

I constantly looked at her picture on my wall and prayed for her health to improve. I was in bad shape, and it seemed like that semester would never end. Finally, the semester was over, and the day came when I was ready to leave for New York. *Oops*, there was just one slight problem. Snow sent me the money for my bus ticket, but she put **CASH** in the envelope and mailed it to me. I never got it! Evidently, a postal worker realized the envelope contained cash and decided they would steal it. So, my father ended

## My Journey

up getting a loan from the bank so I could purchase my ticket to New York. See, he wasn't all bad.

I kept this picture on the wall over my bed.
**I love you, my baby!**

Finally, I arrived in Bronx, New York, and into the arms of my beautiful wife. *Oh, Happy Days!* I spent the summer in New York working at Sealtest Milk Company and saved my money to buy clothes and have some extra money. When we returned to the campus, we had to find a place to live. After Snow and I returned to our college, I ran into my friend, Thurman Gilbert, and told him we were looking for a place to live.

*Gilbert and I both worked as dormitory counselors in Lewis Hall.* Luckily for us, Gilbert, and his wife, Rogenia, had just rented

# My Journey

a house with two bedrooms. He suggested that we all live in the house and split the rent. Snow and I agreed to this arrangement and moved in immediately. This was the beginning of my junior year.

A short time later, Dean Gilmore *(Dean of Students)* allowed Gilbert to live in the **Counselor's Suite** in Lewis Hall *free of charge*. This is the dorm I lived in previously and the same dorm where we both worked. When Gilbert told me he would be moving out of the house we were renting together, I told him I didn't know what I would do because I could not afford to pay the full rent on the house. Gil told me not to worry.

He said the dormitory suite in Lewis Hall had two bedrooms and for me to hold on for about a week to give him time to get in and then he was going to bring us in to stay in the extra bedroom. He said it should not be a problem since we worked in the dormitory as counselors. You see, Gilbert had **clout and influence** on campus and, as a result, received many perks. Snow and I moved into the extra bedroom in a week or so. *(However, Dean Gilmore certainly was not aware of the arrangement!)*

Sadly, around the beginning of the 2$^{nd}$ semester of our junior year (1968), Gilbert and Rogenia divorced. After the divorce, Rogenia moved out and then Gilbert came to me and said he would move out and find somewhere else to live and Snow and

# My Journey

I could keep the counselor's suite. And of course, we still did not have to pay any rent. What a friend! We stayed there for a year without having to pay any rent.

Standing outside our apartment *(Counselor's Suite in Lewis Hall in the background)*. Snow was pregnant with our first son, Michael.

During this time, Snow was pregnant with Mike, and one morning there was NO food to eat and NO money. I remember telling Snow that I did not marry her to have her live like that. I said I would quit school for a while and go downtown and find a job so I could take better care of her.

She looked at me and stated very emphatically, "NO! You are **NOT** going to quit school! We will go hungry together if we don't have anything to eat. But you are NOT going to quit school."

As fate would have it, Gilbert just happened to stop by that day, looked in the refrigerator and playfully asked, "What's on the

## My Journey

menu?" I said, "You're looking at it!" The only thing in the refrigerator was a pie crust and a jug of water. In the cabinets, there was only a can of strawberries.

Gilbert looked at me and said, *"What? Man, your wife is pregnant! We've got to get some food up in here. Let's go."* He had a car, drove me to the grocery store, and bought food for us. THANK YOU, JESUS! I think you are beginning to see why I refer to Gilbert as my brother.

Other than my family, he is the BEST friend I have ever had in my life. **"A true friend steps in when the whole world walks out on you."** Thanks to Gilbert, we made it through that semester.

### MIKE'S ARRIVAL

When school was out for the summer, Snow and I went back to New York anticipating the birth of our first child, Mike. He was born in the Bronx on August 5, 1968, at Lincoln Hospital. I vividly remember the morning Snow went into labor. We were staying with her mom, and it was not yet daybreak and she started telling everyone she was getting ready to have the baby.

Mom asked me to call 911 and get someone to transport her to the hospital. I was so nervous, and when the operator

# My Journey

answered I said to her: "My wife is having a baby! Please send a *hospital!*" After the operator calmed me down, she said she would send the paramedics to take us to Lincoln Hospital in the Bronx.

After arriving at the hospital, the medical staff immediately took Snow away and asked me to sit in the waiting room. They said they would let me know when the baby was born. I waited and no one ever came out to talk to me. Finally, between nine and ten that morning, I called Mom to tell her I had not heard anything from the hospital staff regarding Snow's condition.

That's when Mom told me the hospital had called and informed her Snow had a baby boy! I was very excited but also upset because I was sitting in the waiting room all that time, and NO ONE bothered to come out and let me know my wife had had the baby! I still get angry when I think about it. But then I try to be reasonable. I was only twenty at the time and looked much younger, so the hospital staff probably looked out in the waiting room and never imagined I was the father!

A few weeks after Mike was born, we flew back to Arkansas, and I enrolled in college for my senior year. After returning to the campus, Snow and I continued to stay in the counselor's suite in Lewis Hall. Periodically, during the first semester, Dean Gilmore would stop by the suite looking for

# My Journey

Gilbert, and each time, I would answer the door and inform him Gilbert was not there.

Finally, one day when he stopped by again to see Gilbert, he said, *"Lincoln, are you living here?"* I told him my wife and I did live there, and Gilbert had moved out. He wanted to know if Gilbert was charging me to stay there and I said no. He told me I could stay until the semester ended, but then I would have to move out. I thanked him for allowing us to remain until the end of the semester.

When the semester ended, Snow and I moved out of the counselor's suite and began renting a house with my brother, Bobby, and his wife, Betty. This was my senior year, and Gilbert and I were preparing to begin our student teaching in Brinkley at my old high school. We were going to stay at my home in Brinkley. Many of the students preparing to go off to different school districts to begin their student teaching had gone to the college's Business Office and were given a small loan to help with their expenses. When I heard about this, I immediately went to the business office to get a small loan but was told by the business manager that no more money was available.

Later in the day, I ran into Gilbert, and he asked me if I had gotten any money from the business office. I told him the business

# My Journey

manager informed me that no more money was available. Gilbert said, "Come on, let's go back over there." When we got to the business office, Gilbert got the attention of the business manager and said, "This is Lincoln Butler."

Before he could say anything else, the business manager said, "Yes, I know Lincoln." Gilbert told him we would be staying together at my home while completing our student teaching and I would need some money to get the utilities turned on. The business manager looked over at one of his assistants and said to her, "Give Lincoln Butler $125.00." Gilbert had that kind of clout and status on campus. Everybody knew him.

At some point during this time, my brothers and some other homeboys decided things were getting too tough financially for them on campus. So, they all quit college and left for Flint, Michigan. I hated to see my brothers leave, but I had to stay and finish my education because getting a college degree was NOT an option for me. It was the only way I knew that would allow me to provide a decent life for my wife and my children. So, I stayed! Around this time, I shared "My Vision" for our family with Snow. I told her I envisioned the following:

# My Journey

- **Phase One** of our life should be devoted to preparing ourselves educationally and establishing ourselves in our careers.

- **Phase Two** we would concentrate on our children, ensuring they had what they needed to successfully get through high school and college, and establish themselves in their chosen careers. *(I told Snow this would be a time of great sacrifice to ensure our children were adequately prepared to take care of themselves as adults.)*

- **Phase Three – IT'S OUR TIME!** I remember telling Snow if we successfully navigated phases one and two, we should be able to really enjoy our lives in phase three. This would be a time to travel, enjoy our grandchildren, and do whatever our hearts desired. Phase Three would be *"Our Time!"*

**STUDENT TEACHING**

During the spring semester of 1969, Gilbert and I moved into my family home at 409 Union Street in Brinkley, Arkansas, to begin our Student Teaching at the high school I graduated from. I was assigned to teach social studies and Gilbert taught English. Shortly after we moved into the family home, daddy showed up

# My Journey

one evening. *(Remember, Bobby and I had gone to Brinkley sometime earlier to make sure he was NOT living in **mama's house** with his new family.)*

Anyway, when he came into the house, he started ranting and raving about the fact that Gilbert could not stay there. He said if he could not stay there with his family, then Gilbert could not stay there. This was another time I had to stand my ground with my father. I tried to explain to daddy who Gilbert was and how much he had helped me in the past, and we were completing our "required" student teaching at the high school. He still wanted to raise hell, so I simply told him **Gilbert was NOT leaving. Period!** He got the message and left.

A day or so after that happened, Gilbert and I had gotten home from school and were watching the news on TV when daddy walked in. He didn't say a word. He just walked over to the TV and unplugged it. When we protested, he said, "This is MY TV, and WE have to have something to watch!" So, away he went with the TV. What could I say? It was HIS TV!

Overall, I think I had a very successful student-teaching experience, if you don't count the first day I took over the classes. Shortly after my supervising teacher left the room, one of my seniors got angry with me and jumped up from his desk, put his

# My Journey

fists up, and took a fighting stance because I had asked him to read a section of the social studies text. Oh boy, the college of education had NOT prepared me for this situation. Not sure what would have happened if one of my students hadn't run to alert my supervising teacher who returned immediately.

He took over the situation, and needless to say, I was relieved. Later, I learned this was a troubled student who was known to give everyone a hard time. I also learned he was illiterate and felt as if I had embarrassed him in front of the class. The student was suspended from school, but instead of leaving the campus, he found a huge stick and went and sat on the "roof" of my supervising teacher's car with his feet resting on the hood. The principal, a very large man, went outside and demanded that he leave the campus immediately, which he did.

NOTE: While completing my student teaching, my supervising teacher resigned for a higher-paying job with the railroad. The district then signed me on as the 'teacher of record' to finish the semester with pay. I also signed a contract to teach there the following school year.

# My Journey

# My Journey

## Chapter VIII: Living and Teaching In Brinkley, AR

**MARIAN ANDERSON HIGH SCHOOL**

I was 21 years old when I signed my first teaching contract for a total of $5,508 *for the entire year!* I began my teaching career at Marian Anderson High School in Brinkley, Arkansas, where I graduated from high school. This was quite exciting for me to join the teaching staff, where many of the teachers who had taught me were still there. Call me crazy, but I bought a brand-new car before receiving my first check. My principal, Mr. Randolph, had connections with the car dealer and co-signed for me to get the car. The monthly payments were $125.00, and my teaching salary was just over $400 per month.

## My Journey

After a few months had passed, I was voted "Teacher of the Month" by the students. I really did enjoy my time teaching in Brinkley, but with that low salary, I was barely meeting my financial obligations. During the spring semester, the principal called for a faculty meeting to discuss our "raise" for the following year. My raise would be $50.00 spread out over the next school year. At that point, I decided to move my family to Flint, Michigan, when the school year ended. I felt very strongly I would earn more money and have better opportunities for growth in a larger city.

Below is a picture of the faculty during the year I taught in Brinkley, and I would like to highlight *(In Bold)* three of my elementary teachers who were still there:

Photo Courtesy of Marian Anderson H. S.
Brinkley Faculty – 1969-1970

# My Journey

Back Row - left to right: Rev. Johnson *(he married us)*, L. Butler, E. Tucker, C. Terrell, L. Randolph (principal), forgot, Baker, L.W. Armstrong, Coach Williams

Seated - left to right: Randolph, Baker, Billings, Williams, Swanigan, **Burton** *(The teacher who whipped me for chasing girls with a stick and then lying about it.)*, **Bryant** *(My favorite elementary teacher.)*, **Truesdale**, forgot, forgot.

## LINC'S ARRIVAL *(Drama with Uncle David!)*

Linc was born on May 2, 1970, in St. Louis, Missouri. I was teaching during the day and did not want Snow to be left alone because it was getting close to the baby's due date. Plus, the hospital in Brinkley left much to be desired. It was very inadequate, to say the least! So, mama encouraged me to bring Snow to St. Louis to stay with her until she had the baby. I remember early one Sunday morning Uncle David came over to my house in Brinkley and woke me up. He said, "Wake up, daddy. Your wife has had the baby!" I was extremely excited! Another baby boy!

Later that day, Uncle David told me we should go to St. Louis and see Snow and the baby. I was hesitant to take the trip to St. Louis because I had to teach school the next day. But eventually, I agreed and that evening we left for St. Louis. When we first left Brinkley, Uncle David was drinking his alcohol and was very cheerful and excited about the trip. But, after some time, I noticed he had stopped drinking and had become very quiet.

# My Journey

He then looked at me and asked, *"Where the hell are you taking me?"* I told him we were on our way to St. Louis, and he was the one who encouraged me to go. He told me to turn around because he was not going to St. Louis. Well, we were probably about halfway at that point and now I am excited about seeing my wife and my new baby boy. So, I told Uncle David to take another drink and relax because we were not going to turn back! He threw the drink bottle under his seat and cussed me out, but I continued to St. Louis.

Along the way, I hit a deer! It was nighttime. I saw the deer up ahead on the side of the highway and assumed it would just run toward the woods as I approached it. But instead, the deer turned and jumped directly into the front side of my car near the right headlight. After I hit the deer, I stopped and backed up and saw the deer was in a crouched position on the side of the highway. We decided it was better and safer for us not to mess with it, so we continued on our way to St. Louis. The right front fender of my car sustained some minor damage.

After arriving in St. Louis, we told Uncle Clarence about the deer, and all he wanted to know was why we didn't just run over it again, put it in the car, and bring it on to St. Louis. He said that was some "good meat" we left on the highway. I told Uncle

# My Journey

Clarence I would not risk tearing my new car up to kill a deer. We all laughed about it. It should be noted as soon as Uncle David said hello to everyone, he started in on me again about taking him back to "Fat." That's what he called his wife. We left the next day.

During the last week of school, I invited Big Daddy and Big Mama *(my father's parents)* to our home in Brinkley to have lunch with Snow and me before we left for Michigan. Even though Snow was somewhat nervous about cooking for my grandparents, I convinced her to prepare a nice lunch for them. She was nervous because everyone knows "Big Mamas" worldwide know how to COOK! But Snow prepared a delicious meal for them, and I remember Big Daddy saying how much it meant to him. He said daddy had never invited him to have a meal at our home. He and Big Mama were proud to eat with us and we were honored to have them. Three cheers to my beautiful, brave wife for meeting the challenge!

Prior to the last day of school, Snow and I had already packed up everything we owned in a U-Haul trailer and had it parked in the driveway. When I got home from school on the last day, I just backed my new Mercury Montego up to the trailer, hooked it up, locked the house, and we were on our way to Flint,

# My Journey

Michigan. We stopped in St. Louis and spent the night with mama and my younger brothers and sisters.

# My Journey

## Chapter IX: Life in Flint, Michigan

I was 22 years old when we arrived in Flint, Michigan, and we stayed with Acy and his wife Pat for a short time until we found a house to rent. I got a job working as a Neighborhood Youth Corp Counselor and my office was located at the Flint Board of Education Administration Building.

One of my main duties was organizing NYC Clubs or groups in the three high schools: Central, Northern, and Southwestern. I then had to find part-time afterschool jobs for all the students and serve as the liaison between the students and the employers, intervening when problems or concerns arose.

This was a "win-win" arrangement for all involved. The employers were happy because after they trained the students, they got free labor. *(My program paid the students.)* The students were happy because they had a job making money, plus they were gaining some valuable work experience. I held regular counseling sessions with the students and took them on field trips. Snow and I lived in Flint for two years: from May 1970-June 1972.

**DIRRICK'S ARRIVAL**

Dirrick was born on August 22, 1971, at New York Hospital in Manhattan, NY. Although we were still living in Flint, Michigan, Snow wanted to go to New York to live with her mom until she had the baby. Mama wanted her to come also because she wanted to help us out. But I did not understand and became upset and said some things I should not have said. I told Snow I felt like she was running out on me when I needed her most. Nothing could be further from reality!

Snow was trying to take some of the expenses off me by staying with mom until Dirrick was born. She felt, in the long run, this would benefit us financially. Now, this is the definition of **"Wisdom:"** *The quality of having experience, knowledge, and good judgment; the quality of being wise.* At that time, I possessed ABSOLUTELY NONE of those traits! I was just a little cocky, hot-headed, immature brat. Well, I lost that battle, and Snow went to New York to stay with her mom.

# My Journey

I remember anxiously waiting for mama to call me and tell me Snow had had the baby. Now, this gets interesting because Snow already had two boys. She just knew she would have a girl this time. She wanted to have a girl so badly she only picked a name for a girl: Kimberly Renee. She also said she knew she would have a girl because Mike stayed close to her and showed her so much attention while carrying Dirrick.

Well, as it turns out, she did not have the little girl she craved; instead, she had another baby boy! WOW! MY THREE SONS! But this is not the end of the story. In as much as Snow was insistent she would have a girl, she did not bother with coming up with any names for a boy. So consequently, Dirrick laid up in the hospital for three days without a name.

His name tag read "Boy-Butler." It was crazy! Snow called back to Flint asking me for a name. Well, I always liked the name Derrick, so we decided that would be his name. Derrick's hospital stay was also extended to about a week due to a "heart murmur" the doctors wanted to check out before releasing him.

By now, you have probably noticed the difference in how I spell Dirrick's name. This is NOT a mistake. You see, when he was born, I named him DERRICK. But the people at the hospital made

# My Journey

a mistake and spelled his name DIRRICK so we never changed it because I don't think we noticed it until later in his life.

While living in Michigan, we bought our FIRST HOME in September 1971 at a small cost of $17,700. Our home was located at 6150 Magnolia Lane, Mt. Morris, Michigan. In December 2019, Snow and I went back to Flint for Fred Marshall's funeral and drove to our old home to reminisce.

The home looked small, and the streets seemed much narrower than I recalled. I remember there was a little girl living next door and Mike would talk to her through the fence. I guess he liked her because he climbed up the fence to speak to her. I suppose he was trying to show her his athletic prowess. Anyway, I noticed one day he had gotten his clothes caught on the wire and could not get down. I ran out and got him off the fence. Well, so much for his courting!

After living in Flint for only two years, Snow and I both realized we were unhappy there. So, in June 1972, we decided to sell our home and move to New York City where most of her family lived.

# My Journey

## Chapter X: Life in "The Big Apple"

I was 24 when I moved my family to New York City. As I mentioned earlier, I had spent most of my summers living and working in New York during college, so I was already familiar with the Big Apple.

I immediately began working at my brother-in-law's *(Gaines)* variety store while preparing to gain employment as a teacher with the New York City Board of Education. I remember the officials at the district headquarters in Brooklyn interviewed me and administered a written test that would allow me to teach with what was known as a "Certificate of Competency" until I could take the National Teacher Examination. **(I will get back to this later!)**

Before I discuss my BATTLE with the National Teacher Examination and my teaching experiences in New York City, I

# My Journey

want to share with you my love for weightlifting which I developed while living in New York.

## WEIGHTLIFTING

Over the years, I developed a love for weightlifting and was quite strong for my size. I always knew I was as strong or stronger than most kids my age, and I always wanted a set of weights. So, after we moved to New York, my wife bought me a beautiful set of weights and that's when I officially began weight training. Sometimes I would stay up most of the night training. I liked the transformation I saw as my body was changing. Man, I was starting to develop real muscles!

This is 110 lbs. (Not a lot of weight but lifting a barbell off the floor with one hand is not easy. You must concentrate on balancing the barbell with one hand as you lift it over your head and then lock your elbow. You must also have very strong hands, which I did.)

# My Journey

I'd still like to be that strong. However, time, age, and lack of exercise significantly change *your body and your life.*

I think I was 26 years old when this picture was taken. Wow! I even had a full head of hair!

# My Journey

I was living in the Bronx when these were taken *(around 1974).*

*Bronx, New York (1974)*

## My Journey

Even though I was small, I don't recall anyone near my size *(and many much larger than me)* lifting more weight than me! I competed against friends, associates, and strangers in New York, New Jersey, St. Louis, Arkansas, and Dallas, and I usually whipped them all!

On one of my visits to St. Louis to see my family, including my cousins Bud and Tommy, they wanted to know if I would compete in weightlifting against a friend of theirs in the neighborhood who also lifted weights. Call me crazy, but I loved lifting weights, and I was also a little cocky and always ready for a challenge.

We all went to his place and the competition was on. This dude was bigger than me and he was quite strong. It seemed like we were about even for quite some time, so we continued to add more weight. We were competing by engaging in different types of lifts such as standing curls, sitting curls, bench presses, squats, sit-ups, etc.

He gave me a good whipping with the squats (I have bad knees, so I was never able to *train my legs properly),* but I tore him up on pretty much all the other lifts as the weight got heavier and heavier! I felt good because my cousins and brothers were cheering me on, and I did not want to disappoint them. After the

# My Journey

competition, the dude "high-fived" and congratulated me. We all laughed, drank beer, and had a great time together!

**Quick Story**

While living on Whitewood Dr. here in Dallas, I remember inviting my brothers, some of my male cousins, and friends over to play basketball and hang out together. Eventually, our attention turned to weightlifting to see who was the strongest. *(This was a male testosterone challenge I couldn't resist)* I beat everyone, so someone added all my weights to the barbell and issued a challenge to see if anyone could bench press it.

I have had a competitive nature as far back as I can remember. Even as a young child, I hated to get beat, no matter the game. So, when the challenge was issued to see who could press the entire bar of weights, I, along with everyone else, proudly accepted the challenge believing we would somehow be able to do it. Well, it seems that we all met our match that day. Each of us tried in seemingly every conceivable way possible to lift the weight, but all were UNSUCCESSFUL!

As the day wore on, everyone had exhausted themselves, so we decided to leave the weights alone. I am sure after everyone went home, they probably never thought about that challenge again. But no, not me and my competitive nature. I could not get it

## My Journey

out of my head, and it bothered me because I was unable to lift that weight!

Up to the time I went to bed, I was still thinking about the weight. As I lay in bed that night, it seemed like the weight started *calling my name*. I continued to toss and turn with the urge to lift that weight getting stronger and stronger. Finally, I got up and went down to the garage where the weights were.

Here's where the story gets scary! **PLEASE DON'T EVER TRY THIS! SERIOUSLY!!!** It was about 2:30 in the morning and I was in the garage *all alone.* My wife and sons were in bed sound asleep. As long as I had been lifting weights, I knew better than to attempt to lift heavy, dead weights without a spotter. I really don't think I was planning to try lifting the weight since we had all failed miserably that afternoon. Eventually, I laid down on the bench, started feeling around on the weight and made small attempts to lift it straight up.

Finally, I got the nerve to lift it off the rack but quickly guided it back onto the rack. After lying there for a few moments, I decided to lift it straight up again. For the life of me, I still don't know what got into me, but I brought the weights down until the bar was a few inches above my chest.

# My Journey

Oh Crap! What the heck was I thinking? Here I am, *all alone* in the garage at 2:30 in the morning, with this tremendously heavy weight hovering a few inches above my chest. Remember, ALL of us failed at every attempt during the afternoon to lift the weight. But it was crunch time now. There was no one to turn to and I was NOT planning on going out like that. So, I immediately attempted to raise the weight back up but couldn't do it.

Now I'm thinking, oh my God, it's PRAYING TIME! I need HELP! To make a long story short, I remember how scared I was after realizing there was *no one* in the garage to help me. Someone said to me later, why didn't you rest the weight on your chest and roll it off?

Well, they obviously don't know much about lifting heavy weights. You see, if I had allowed that weight to rest on my chest in an attempt to "roll" it off me, it would have crushed my rib cage and my lungs. No, I only had one way out of this harrowing situation: to somehow lift that weight back up and into the rack.

You know, earlier, I said I was *all alone* in the garage, but now, I know someone else was in the garage with me. Praise be to God! Even though I had made several unsuccessful attempts to get that weight off me, something told me to try one more time.

# My Journey

I did not hear this voice with my ears, but in my spirit, it was loud and clear. IT HAD TO BE THE VOICE OF GOD. For it is only by His grace and mercy that I can sit here today and tell this story.

Miraculously, I listened to the voice, made one more attempt, lifted that weight up, and placed it back onto the rack. Hallelujah!! TO GOD BE THE GLORY! I will forever be thankful and grateful. I believe God rescued me from that frightening ordeal because I had not completed my destiny here on Earth. Thank you, Jesus, for your love and your mercy! Then I quickly got the heck out of that garage!!! Oh, and by the way, I am labeling this one **INSANE!**

*Two Lessons Learned:*
1) *Never attempt to lift heavy weights without a spotter!*
2) *Remember, God is able!*


**My Bench Press results at the Nolan Estes Plaza for the 30-39 age group:**

# My Journey

January 20, 1984

CONGRATULATIONS !!!

... on your top performance at the Plaza during our DISD Wellness Program assessments this fall.

Your **bench press** total of **244 lbs.** was the **best** for men/~~women~~ in your age group tested at the Plaza.

I am planning to post a "Best Performance Board" at the Plaza to recognize such great achievements like yours. Each name will be displayed by age group like this:

| age group | name | score |
|---|---|---|
| 30-39 | Lincoln Butler | 244 |

and will remain until someone else in your age group "tops" your mark.

Ironically, my favorite Bible Verse is, and has always been, Philippians 4:13 — *"I can do all things through Christ who strengthens me."* Throughout my college days and my employment years, whenever I was faced with seemingly insurmountable obstacles *(including lifting heavy weights)*, I always recited this verse over and over in my mind as I worked diligently to succeed at whatever the task or challenge might be. God is good!

Now, back to the NATIONAL TEACHER EXAMINATION. That *bad boy* gave me a run for my money. The first time I took the National Teacher Examination, I did not study and prepare for it; consequently, I failed one part of the two-part test. I only missed it by a few points, but never-the-less, I failed!

# My Journey

The second time I did try to prepare myself by studying more and spending most of the time preparing for the part of the test I failed the first time around.

Well, the day of the test rolled around and what did I do? I went to work in the Bronx and taught school all day. Then, I had to get in my car and drive to Brooklyn in the evening rush-hour traffic! In New York City, every hour seems like "rush-hour," so it was a torturous drive to Brooklyn. It also didn't help that I was running out of time to get there before the start of the test.

After reaching the test site, I could not find a parking place, and the clock was ticking. I had to park quite a distance from the building where the test was being administered. So, I jumped out of the car, and it was "off to the races." As I approached the testing room door, the test administrator was closing the door but saw me and allowed me to come in. Everyone was calmly seated as I entered the room and looked as if they were ready to PASS the test. Well, I was a sweaty mess and nervous because I barely made it into the room. If I had been a few seconds later, I would not have been able to enter the testing room.

After all of this, I did not have a good feeling about taking the test, and yes, I failed it AGAIN! Only this time, I passed the part I had failed the first time and failed the part I had passed the

## My Journey

first time. Again, I only missed passing by a very few points. Now I'm wondering, what do I have to do to get this "monkey off my back?" After I got my test results back, my supervisor called me to see how I had done.

I was highly embarrassed to inform him I had failed it again. He asked me about the test day, and I shared with him I had worked that day and then drove to Brooklyn and the traffic was very bad. Then I couldn't find parking near the test site and ended up having to run like crazy to get to the testing room just as they were closing the door. I told him after experiencing all that frustration before the beginning of the test, I was already feeling defeated!

My supervisor's name was Mr. Henry May. Instead of trying to put me down and make me feel stupid, he lifted me up and encouraged me. He said, "First, you are going to have to set aside some quality time for preparation because it's been a while since you were in school; then, on the day of the test, you are NOT going to go to work. Instead, you will go to Brooklyn early enough to find a good parking space and relax before going into the testing site." He then assured me that I was smart and just needed to settle down and I would pass the test.

## My Journey

Well, I registered for this test for the third time and spent quite a bit of time studying and preparing for success. I also stayed home from work and got to Brooklyn early that day, so I would not have to deal with as much traffic. As we began the test, I did have a different mindset and felt really good after completing the test. Even so, I still remember how I felt when I got my test results for the third time. I was so nervous, and I was afraid to open the envelope.

Finally, I got enough nerve to open it and slowly pulled the document out. I nearly fainted! All I saw was **PASS! PASS!** I had finally passed both parts of the National Teacher Examination! To God Be the Glory! It truly felt like the weight of the world had been lifted off my shoulders. I am so thankful Mr. May understood what I was going through, shared his wisdom, and coached me to VICTORY! *Lesson Learned: NEVER GIVE UP. Be willing to fight for what you want in this life for yourself and your family.*

I was determined to pass that test! I was NOT going to allow one test to determine my destiny and the future I had dreamed about for my wife and sons! NO WAY! Passing that test was my ticket to a better life for my family. There was NO WAY I was going to give up! As Bishop T. D. Jakes said, *"A setback is a setup for a comeback!"*

# My Journey

I hate to even think about what type of life I would have had if I had given up on my teaching career. Remember, due to my eye injury, I had lost out on job opportunities. The military had also rejected me. Brother Malcolm X said, *"**Education** is our passport to the future. For tomorrow belongs only to those who prepare for it today."*

I quickly realized my own *"personal passport to the future"* would be through EDUCATION, and thanks to God, it has served my family and me well. Since passing that test, I have never looked back and have done some amazing things in my career and life.

However, I never made much money; teachers and principals didn't make much money in those days. But after I passed the test, I never had to worry about how I would care for my wife and my children because there was always a demand for **good** teachers. And let's be honest, it's not always about the most money.

This may sound like a cliché, but there's a tremendous amount of joy and fulfillment in knowing you are touching the lives of many children in a positive way as a teacher. You have an opportunity to influence their decisions to positively impact their lives.

# My Journey

I have watched many former students become teachers, principals, central office administrators, college professors, curriculum writers, accountants, professional boxers, doctors, lawyers, district attorneys, etc. It has been very rewarding!

I often referred to the poem "Don't Quit" by Edgar A. Guest when faced with obstacles along my journey. If you have ever thought about giving up on your dreams when facing challenges, then I encourage you to also remember Abraham Lincoln's Journey to the Presidency:

| | |
|---|---|
| 1832 | Defeated for State Legislature |
| 1833 | Failed in Business |
| 1838 | Defeated for Speaker |
| 1843 | Defeated for Nomination for Congress |
| 1848 | Lost Renomination for Congress |
| 1854 | Defeated for U.S. Senate |
| 1856 | Defeated for Nomination for Vice President |
| 1858 | Again Defeated for U.S. Senate |
| 1860 | Elected President of the United States |

*LESSON LEARNED: "Your desire for success should be greater than your fear of failure."* Azie Morton Taylor

During my career, I also used my personal experiences, the failures and the triumphs, to help guide and motivate many of my teachers to victory, as Mr. May had done with me. I was never too

## My Journey

proud to share with them some of the challenges I faced but refused to give up! Over the years, many teachers have thanked me for sharing my experiences with them and for not letting them give up because of testing difficulties or other obstacles.

**TEACHING IN NEW YORK CITY**

I was hired by the New York City Board of Education to teach in a special reading program called Youth Tutoring Youth. This was a unique instructional arrangement where students were brought together for one class period daily in small groups consisting of one sixth-grade student (tutor) and two fourth-grade students (tutees) for "tutorial sessions." A tutorial session involved up to twenty-four students in a room at a time (8 groups of 3 students) working as independent tutor/tutee "cores." In addition to the tutorial sessions, workshops were scheduled for tutors only. I was the "Teacher in Charge", with two-four Educational Assistants and one Student Aide working in the classroom.

# My Journey

Two of my Outstanding Youth Tutoring Youth Staff Members: Dorothy Brisbon & Barbara Jackson *(with Lincoln Butler)*

One of the main reasons I enrolled in graduate school and got my master's degree was because I had been denied various positions in New York that required a master's degree. Then I ran across this quote from Whitney M. Young in one of my books: *"It is better to be prepared and NOT wanted than to be wanted and NOT prepared."*

Some of those employers wanted to hire me but I lacked the preparation required for the job. I did not have an advanced degree. At this point, I was determined not to be caught in that position again. That's when I enrolled in graduate school, and since I was teaching reading, I decided to get my masters in reading so that I would know what the heck I was doing!

# My Journey

At the end of my first year of teaching in New York, I had not passed the National Teacher Exam (NTE), so I did not report back to the campus where I had been teaching because I didn't think I had a job. Plus, I never received any school opening letter or correspondence from the school announcing when to report or anything like that.

So, even though I wanted to teach, I didn't think I had a job anymore. *(I guess it never occurred to me to go to the school before school began and speak with the principal about my situation with the NTE.)* My Mistake! BIG MISTAKE! Hey, I was young, naïve, and very inexperienced and I didn't know any better.

After completing my application to enroll in graduate school for the fall semester, I needed a letter of recommendation from my former principal. I went to the school to ask the principal for a recommendation, thinking she would be proud of me for enrolling in graduate school.

This was during the fall of 1974. Instead, she made me wait for a very long time before finally calling me into her office. She was angry with me, and boy, she let me know. She said, *"You've got a lot of nerve coming back here asking me for a letter of recommendation. I had saved a position for you, and even if you were not planning to teach this year, you should have had the*

# My Journey

*decency to let me know."* She didn't even give me an adequate opportunity to explain to her what had happened and why I did not show up at the beginning of the school year. She simply said, *"No, I will NOT give you a letter of recommendation! I am going to teach you people about **burning your bridges**!"* She then ESCORTED ME OUT OF HER OFFICE!

I left there traumatized, baffled, and embarrassed, not really understanding what had just happened. I didn't see that coming! I don't think I ever saw or heard from her again. *Despite that principal's refusal to give me a recommendation, I was still able to enroll in graduate school. I got off to a great start completing my master's degree with a 3.90 GPA.* I might also add that it was a black female principal who treated me this way.

In retrospect, I honestly can see why she was upset with me, and **she was right**. I was dealing with the shame and embarrassment of failing the test and didn't even think about going to the school to see if I could continue teaching until I received a passing score. As I said, this was a big mistake, and I learned a huge lesson from this experience! I only wish she had handled it with more dignity and professionalism.

This is the first school where I taught while living in New York. *This is also the school where the principal escorted me from her office!*

# My Journey

*Public School #132 – My 1st teaching assignment in NY!!*

This is the second campus where I taught in New York: The principal was Ms. Audrey B. O'Neal, and she was extremely kind and supportive. I really enjoyed my two years with her.

*Public School #63 – My 2nd teaching assignment in NY!*

My program at this campus was very successful and ended up serving as the *model school site* for the Youth Tutoring Youth Program. Then, three years into my teaching tenure in the NYC school system, disaster struck. The YTY Program and many others were cut due to the "fiscal" problems besetting New York City.

# My Journey

This caused the school district to relinquish many of its fine achievement programs. I was laid off from my teaching job after the program was cut.

Now, I was at a crossroads in my life. I no longer had a job teaching, and I was right in the middle of my graduate program. Not to mention I had to care for a wife and three little children. I contemplated quitting graduate school because I wasn't teaching, and I didn't think it made much sense to continue this degree program in education, majoring in corrective reading. I remember discussing my dilemma with my mother and she said, *"Lincoln, you may not be able to use that master's degree right now but look at it as an **investment** in your future! Stay in school if you can."* I remained in graduate school and continued to work at my brother-in-law's store.

Eventually, I was employed by the **New York City Housing Authority as a Recreation Director at James Monroe Community Center.** I worked at Monroe Center from the fall of 1975 until the fall of 1976, thinking I might get called back to continue teaching. However, instead of re-hiring the teachers who had been laid off, the school district was forced to lay off even more teachers. I spoke with former colleagues, and some were thinking of quitting because they had more than forty students in their

## My Journey

classes due to the cutbacks. They didn't even have enough desks for the students, and some had to sit on the windowsills.

In August 1976, I completed my master's degree. Since I did not get called back to teach, I decided it was time to move my family out of New York City. Additionally, I wanted to get my sons out of this big city while they were still very young.

**Dirrick, Lincoln, Jr., and Michael**

I felt like they would have a better chance of growing up successfully in a different city. New York City has so much to offer, but also many distractions which could easily take the focus off your life goals. As I was finishing my last graduate courses, one of my graduate school professors, who knew that many of us had been released from our teaching jobs, informed the class about places in the country where teachers were in demand. Dallas, Texas, was on the list. I had never been to Texas but my wife's

# My Journey

brothers, Prince and Fred, were already living in Dallas. So, I packed my clothes and began preparing for my long solo journey to Texas!

## GOAL-SETTING

Before I left New York, I sat with my wife and discussed the following goals I had prepared for myself:

- **Immediate Goal** – Travel to Dallas and secure a teaching position. *I was pleased that this goal was accomplished without any complications.*
- **Intermediate Goal** – Send for my wife and children to join me in Dallas. *Shortly after I started teaching, my wife and children joined me in Dallas. Mission Accomplished!*
- **Long Range Goal** – Enroll in a graduate program for educational administration and supervision and obtain my mid-management certification for the principalship. *Mission Accomplished!*
- **Ultimate Goal** – Secure an administrative assignment within five-seven years with plans to eventually become a **principal.** *Mission Accomplished!*

*Lesson Learned: Remember the importance of Goal-Setting!*

I remember how sad I became leading up to my departure from New York. The very thought of having to leave my family in New York City was truly heartbreaking. But this was a trip that I had to take alone. My duty as a father and husband was to prepare

# My Journey

the way for my family so we could have a chance at a "better life." Late one Saturday night, after my sons were sound asleep, I kissed each of them and told them I loved them. For obvious reasons, I didn't want them to see me leave.

I then embraced my beautiful wife, kissed her, told her how much I loved her, and assured her that I would go and get a job and then send for her and the boys. With tears rolling down my face, I got in my Chevy Vega and headed for the expressway. This was about 11:00 pm, October 2, 1976, one of the saddest days of my life. I was 28 years old, but I had to do what I had to do!

To be accurate, I had two destinations in mind when I left New York: Move back to Flint, Michigan, or travel to Dallas, Texas, and start a new life there. Snow and I really did not want to move back to Flint. And after arriving and spending the weekend there, I was quickly reminded of why I had moved away the first time. So, on Monday morning, when everyone got in their cars and headed to work, I got in my car and headed for Dallas! I stopped in Brinkley, Arkansas, and spent a couple of nights with my mother before I journeyed to Dallas.

# My Journey

## Chapter XI: Dallas, Texas

Before I arrived in Dallas, I had this crazy notion that everyone in Texas rode horses and were basically cowboys. Boy, I was pleasantly surprised when I hit the city limits! Coming from Bronx, New York, where many apartment buildings were run-down, dilapidated structures with trash and litter everywhere, everything in Dallas seemed so modern and clean. I remember calling Snow and telling her how impressed I was with Dallas. I told her it seemed as though everyone owned *a brick house with a two-car garage*. I said, "Snow, there's something good happening here and I am going to get in on it!"

**TEACHING OPPORTUNITIES IN DALLAS**

I remember the day I went down to the school district's administration building and completed an application for teaching.

# My Journey

The personnel officer who interviewed me was Ms. Burlene Durley. She was impressed with my credentials and assured me I would not have any trouble getting hired. She also pointed out that having a master's degree in reading was a plus for me because there was a big push to raise student achievement in reading. *(Thank you, mama, for encouraging me to stay in school and complete my master's degree.)*

Before I left the administration building, the personnel officer called several principals and told them about me, and all wanted to meet with me *ASAP*! Ms. Durley also took me around the administration building and introduced me to several employees while bragging about me.

Ironically, I didn't have a job teaching when I left New York. Now, I get to Dallas and every principal I interviewed with wanted to hire me. Wow, a black man with a master's degree in reading. I was in demand! *(Remember, mama said this would be an investment in my future! How right she was. Hallelujah!)* While I had several schools to choose from, I accepted a teaching position at **W. W. Bushman Elementary School**.

# My Journey

**W. W. Bushman Elementary School**
(Renamed "Albert C. Black Elementary School" in May 2021)

## W. W. BUSHMAN ELEMENTARY SCHOOL

(November 1976-June 1983)

I chose this school mainly because the principal was friendly yet professional and business-like. Plus, he was young and energetic and seemed genuinely interested in having me at his school. He also suggested that he would be very supportive of me and my future goals, which included becoming an administrator one day. The principal assigned me two sections of sixth-grade language arts and social studies classes. The current teacher was being reassigned. He then asked if I could come back on Friday and spend the day observing before taking over the following Monday. I was excited to have an opportunity to observe the classes before officially taking over.

I sat in the classroom the entire day observing and taking notes on Friday. The teacher I was replacing told the kids I would

# My Journey

become their teacher on Monday. She then said she wanted to tell me some things about them. She said the students were out of control and disrespectful and this was her chance to "get them back!" She had each student stand one by one and then berated them. She went up one side of them and down the other. She called them a bunch of losers! As I observed the bewildered look on the faces of the students, I was appalled and stunned that a "so-called" professional educator would demean children that way. I was embarrassed for them. But since these were still her students, there wasn't much I could do. I was not expecting this, and I could barely wait for Monday to come so that I could do my best to redeem the "self-worth" of these precious children.

Standing in the hallway next to my classroom door on Monday morning, I warmly greeted the students as they entered the classroom. After they were all seated and the roll had been called, I formally introduced myself to them and shared a little about my life. They were curious and asked lots of questions about New York and other places where I had lived and taught school. I then said to them that I needed to get to know them and find out some things about each of them.

They quickly reminded me their "other teacher" had already told me about them. I said to them sometimes I have this

# My Journey

problem of NOT remembering things I don't want to hear. I told them I didn't remember ANYTHING the other teacher had told me about them. I then had each of them stand and tell me what *THEY* wanted me to know about them, including their name; whether or not they liked school and why; their favorite subject/least favorite subject; what they aspired to be as an adult; and anything else they wanted to share with me. As they spoke, I took notes.

At first, they were a little hesitant to say much until they realized I honestly wanted to hear what they had to say. After completing this activity, everyone was relaxed, smiling, and feeling better about themselves. I felt good too and knew I had already begun connecting with them.

My students' self-confidence grew by leaps and bounds as the semester progressed! They began working extremely hard and I started telling them "They were #1!" I entered my students in every little contest or activity the school sponsored. We ended up winning EVERYTHING. We won 1st Place in the Spelling Bee; 1st Place in the Oratorical Contest; 1st Place in the Spring Door Decorating Contest, etc. They worked hard!

My students became so confident *and maybe even a little cocky* to the point the principal asked me what in the world I had done to them? He said they were all up in his face telling him they

# My Journey

were the #1 students in the school! These were the same students who, earlier in the year, had been labeled **"A Bunch of Losers!"** I think this dramatic shift in their attitudes and performance had something to do with the following:

    a. Experiencing genuine love and concern from their teacher, maybe for the first time,

    b. Being made to feel special and worthwhile.

    c. Finding ways to make positive connections with them, individually and collectively,

    d. Providing opportunities for **each of them** to experience varying degrees of success,

    e. Praising and encouraging them for their efforts,

    f. Letting them know that it's okay to make mistakes,

    g. Standing up for them when they were right; holding them accountable when they were wrong, etc.

*LESSON LEARNED: Look for the good in your students. An ounce of gold is covered by tons of dirt, but we don't look for the dirt. We look for the gold. My challenge to all teachers and parents is to find the gold in each child.*

# My Journey

As a classroom teacher, I always encouraged my students to **Dream Big Dreams**, and I used myself as an example. Even though I was in the early years of my career and had not been in Dallas very long, I told my students one day they would return to the school with their children, and I would be the principal. Some years later, during student registration, one of my former students was enrolling her child, and she saw me and came over to talk. She was so excited I was there and during our conversation, she reminded me of what I told them. Can you believe it? I was her sixth-grade teacher, and now she was enrolling her child at the same school, and I was now the PRINCIPAL, just like I had told them! *Lesson Learned: Dreams do come true, but you must also be willing to put in the WORK!*

Whenever I would observe or hear teachers complaining about certain students and indicating they did not want them in their classroom, I would often inform the principal that moving them to my class would be okay. I felt then, as I do now, all children need and deserve an opportunity to experience some degree of success in school. I was always willing to give them that opportunity!

Also, when I was a teacher, I would share my desire to become a principal with my colleagues. They would immediately

# My Journey

shut me down and try to discourage me. Then one day, during my planning period, Mrs. Novella Jackson, a math teacher and one of my strong supporters, came into my room and closed the door behind her. When she closed the door, I knew I was in for something. I just didn't know what. She walked over to me and began admonishing me by saying she knew I wanted to become a principal.

She told me to shut my mouth and stop telling the people at the school about my dreams. She said they did not have any dreams of their own and did not want to see me succeed. Further, she said they would do whatever they could to try to make sure I failed. She told me to stop talking and go on and follow my dreams and before they realize it, I will be their boss! I don't know if she was a prophet, but it came true! After a few short years, I became the principal of that school. and many of the naysayers were still there. How about that! To my credit, I did not let them discourage me.

*LESSON LEARNED: "Belief in yourself far outweighs the doubts of others."*

## CLASS 6A

While teaching at Bushman, I had the privilege of working with some very dynamic students, and Class 6A was filled with

# My Journey

some really talented kids. They were extremely smart, and I held them to very high standards. Late in the spring semester of my second year, while standing in the hall during class changes, some of my students in Class 6A were walking around interacting with each other. They all knew when they entered "our" classroom, everyone must be seated and working on the morning assignment, now called a "Bell Ringer."

Whenever I observed this off-task behavior, I would stare at them, and they would quickly find their seats. This particular day I got a little gruff with them because of this behavior and they begged me to *please* let them do what they were doing because it was very important. They emphasized they would make sure all their work was completed. They said, "Mr. Butler, we are working on something special, and we are almost finished with it." Because I had some very good students, I gave them the space to complete whatever it was. I certainly didn't have a clue!

A week or so later, as I stood in front of the students to get the class started for the day, one of my students, Traci Dunn, said to me, "Sit down, Mr. Butler." I said, "Excuse me!" I thought she had lost her mind telling *me* to sit down. Then she said pleadingly, "Mr. Butler, please sit down. We have something for you."

# My Journey

Confused and still without a clue as to what was happening, I complied and took my seat.

At that moment, one of my students, Kathy, began slowly approaching my desk with her hands behind her back. All the other students were starting to assemble behind her. Some were smiling and some had tears in their eyes. As Kathy reached my desk, she removed her hands from behind her back and revealed a beautiful little plaque. She then began making her presentation: Paraphrasing, she said, *"Mr. Butler,* **Class 6A** *of W. W. Bushman would like to present you with this Wisdom Words Award for always being so positive and sharing your words of encouragement and support with us."* She said, *"We know sometimes we gave you a hard time and got on your nerves, but you never gave up on us, and for that we thank you."*

Traci Dunn then added that all those mornings that I had to remind them to get back in their seats and complete their assignments, they were busy collecting portions of their *lunch money* from each other to raise enough money to purchase the plaque. *(Traci's dad had gone out and picked up a plaque for me at the request of the students. I should add that the students designed and paid for it.)* By this time, I, along with my students,

# My Journey

was crying. I mean some of us were balling! This gesture of love and gratitude touched me to the very core of my soul.

Receiving this plaque from my students was very significant and special in and of itself. This was the *first* plaque I had ever received in my professional career, and to think, it was purchased by my students and then presented to me in such a special way. Secondly, they had sacrificed some of their lunch money to pay for it. Finally, and most meaningful, of all the students who could have presented me with the plaque, they chose Kathy to do the honors. Now, let me explain why this is so special. As the school year progressed, I knew I had connected with each of my students, except Kathy. She gave me a run for my money. I mean she tried my last nerve!

And now, Kathy was standing in front of me *smiling* and presenting me with the most meaningful gift I had ever received. It was as if she was saying, *"I know I gave you a hard time, but you never gave up on me. And for that I thank you. Oh, and yes, you CONNECTED with me too!"* When Kathy finished her presentation, I was no good for the rest of the day. I must have cried on and off until the end of the school day! That was forty-four years ago, and I still have that plaque. Yes, I still get a little teary-eyed

## My Journey

when I think about the love those precious children demonstrated toward me that day.

I was fortunate to be recognized with many accolades, awards, plaques, etc., for my work during my career as an educator. But none of them is as special to me as the one from MY PRECIOUS STUDENTS from **Class 6A** of W. W. Bushman Elementary School!

Many of my students from that class have become entrepreneurs, teachers, nurses, doctors, etc. I want to highlight three of them:

**Traci Dunn-Carney** *(Medical Doctor)*

Traci was always an Honor Student. She was simply gifted! During Traci's senior year in high school, the Dallas Independent School District held an awards program for the most outstanding

# My Journey

and esteemed graduating seniors, and of course, Traci was one of those selected. The students were asked to invite **the teacher** who had had the most influence and impact on their lives.

Traci said I was that special teacher in her life, and she invited me to be with her at the awards program. Of all the teachers she had known from kindergarten through twelfth grade, she invited me. What an honor!

In April 2012, I was inducted into the African American Education Archives and History Program's Hall of Fame. Traci attended the ceremony to support me, and during my acceptance remarks, I was extremely proud to introduce her to the audience as **Dr. Traci Dunn-Carney, MD!!!** I also attended a reception for Traci when she was awarded her medical degree in 2007.

**Booker Kidd** *(Professional Boxer)*

Booker became a professional boxer, and I was happy to be able to attend one of his boxing matches. Booker was outstanding and possessed the skills to deliver some wicked "body shots" against his opponent. That night he easily won the match with a TKO. Booker went on to win major awards and titles during his career.

# My Journey

**Anthony Leonard** *(Dallas Police Officer)*

My wife and I were in a restaurant eating one day when I noticed this group of young ladies constantly whispering and staring in my direction. I wasn't sure what was happening, but I thought it was somewhat disrespectful that they would do this with my wife sitting with me.

This continued until we finished our meal and got up to leave. As we walked past their table, one of them stopped me and said, ``Aren't you Mr. Lincoln Butler?" When I said yes, I am, they all started laughing and telling me they were my former sixth-grade students. As they began to introduce themselves, amazingly, I remembered them too.

As we laughed and reminisced, they recalled some of our *specific* classroom activities. Can you believe this? It had been more than 30 years since they were my students, yet they could remember some of the activities we did together at Bushman. The weird thing is I remembered the activities too! It was great seeing them, and they said they enjoyed being in my class.

During our surprise meeting, we talked about many of the students from Class 6A and one of the students they mentioned was Anthony Leonard. They told me Anthony was a Dallas Police Officer.

# My Journey

As fate would have it, shortly after our meeting, I was shopping at my local grocery store and walked upon this guy with his children. He stood there, looked at me, and said, "Excuse me, are you Mr. Butler?"

I said yes, I am. And when he began to smile, Immediately, I recognized him too! This was Anthony Leonard, my little sixth-grade student standing in front of me as this "BIG" muscular gentleman with his children.

We hugged and expressed how good it was to see each other. I told him about meeting some other students from his class a few weeks earlier. Also, during my conversation with Anthony, we discovered that we live right down the street from each other. Anthony introduced me to his children and told them I was the best teacher he had ever had. What an awesome compliment!

As I reflect on my career, I realize these young scholars and their classmates helped shape me into the educator I ultimately became. They will always occupy a special place in my heart, and it is still an honor to call them ***my students!***

# My Journey

Standing: 3rd from left-Booker Kidd-Became a Professional Boxer. 4th from left-Anthony Leonard-Became a Dallas Police Officer

Front Row: 3rd from left
Traci Dunn Carney-Medical Doctor

**NOTE: I STILL REMEMBER MOST OF THESE STUDENTS' NAMES.**

Before Larry died, I was still teaching at Bushman, and I frequently talked to him about wanting to become a school

# My Journey

principal one day. Larry thought this was a good idea and constantly encouraged me to do it. He said he could see me doing a good job as principal. So, during the summer of 1978, I enrolled in graduate school and began working on my administrative certification to become a principal.

I completed two courses that summer and received an "A" in both. That fall of 1978, I enrolled in two more courses, but for some reason, I began feeling weird sitting in that first class. I couldn't concentrate. I sat there thinking about "getting the heck out of there" as soon as we were given a break. So, when the professor gave us our break, I grabbed my book and other documents and headed for my car! That was the end of my schooling for that year.

When Larry died tragically in June of 1979, I had made up my mind that I was NOT going back to school. However, during the summer of 1980, I decided to enroll in two classes. Once again, when the professor gave us our break, I grabbed my book and tablet and darted for the exit. Honestly, after Larry died, I was just "messed up" and was in no shape to return to school. It seems like a part of me died that day along with my brother. *(For a long time, I quietly blamed myself for his death because I kept thinking if I*

# My Journey

*had not questioned Larry and Israel about how to ride a motorcycle, he would not have gotten on it.)*

During the spring of 1981, I began thinking about how Larry had always encouraged me and said he could *see me* being a principal. So, I used his words of encouragement to motivate myself to enroll in two classes, and this time, with Larry's help, I was determined to stay in school and complete my certification in his honor. Whenever I began thinking about quitting, I would think about Larry's words. This kept me going and I stayed in school and completed my administrative certification in the spring of 1982 with a GPA of 3.82. This was the fulfillment of my **Long-Range Goal**.

I remained at W. W. Bushman Elementary School for seven years (1976-1983) in the following capacities: classroom teacher, skills development teacher, Title 1 reading teacher, and administrative intern. I was also named *"Teacher of the Year"* while at Bushman. Below is a letter from one of my former Bushman students and one from one of my Bushman colleagues:

*"I am a former student of Mr. Butler. He came to Bushman in 1976 and I was also new to Bushman that year. Mr. Butler showed interest in our class, and he respected us as a whole, as well as individuals. He made the class fun, exciting, and made it worth our while.*

# My Journey

*Mr. Butler was, and still is, very much the manly image in my life. He gives me many inspiring words of encouragement. He is a man of his word. I was unfortunate to be fatherless, but fortunate to have known Mr. Butler."* **Johnny C., Former Student**

*"Lincoln Butler has literally saved the lives of many children. One child in particular, who stuttered, through Lincoln Butler's skill and caring, went on to win third place in the Oratorical Contest. Another child, emotionally traumatized because her father murdered her mother, could hardly function. Through Mr. Butler's diligence in working with her, she found new meaning in her life. This child won first place in the Oratorical Contest. Mr. Butler came to Bushman in the middle of the term. He inherited a class that considered themselves "losers." Needless to say, they got a handle on self-esteem and consequently, had the most participants and the most winners in the Spelling Bee."*

*"Self-esteem and self-worth are two attributes that Lincoln Butler brings out of his students. Mr. Butler is a good co-worker, always sharing his knowledge, time, and materials with others. Mr. Butler is always excited about what he is doing with his classes. Lincoln Butler is a great teacher, a warm, caring, and a fantastic human being."* **Lorraine J., Music Teacher**

**B. F. DARRELL ELEMENTARY SCHOOL**

# My Journey

(August 1983-July 1984)

During the summer of 1983, I was promoted to assistant principal at B. F. Darrell Elementary School. When school began, the principal and I conducted staff development for the first three days. During this time, I quickly and quietly learned the names of all the teachers. While conducting one of my presentations, I told the teachers I had learned all their names. Certainly, they didn't believe me and immediately challenged me to name each of them. I went through the entire staff, reciting each of their last names and did not miss a single one. The teachers, and my principal, were very impressed.

Just as I was about to continue with my presentation, one of the teachers yelled out, "It's great that you were able to call each of us by our last names, but I bet you don't know our first names!" I said to her, "Actually, I do!" Well, what did I say that for? They challenged me to go down the line and call everyone by their first and last name. I welcomed this challenge because I knew I could do it. After I completed this challenge, they all stared at me like I was from *outer space* or some other planet. I remember the principal saying my "stock" had gone way up with her! She said as long as she had been at Darrell, she could not do what I had just done! Man, you talk about getting off to a GREAT start!

# My Journey

## Chapter XII: The Principalship & Other Admin Assignments

I enjoyed my time as assistant principal at B. F. Darrell. Still, after only *one year*, the superintendent promoted me to the **PRINCIPALSHIP** and reassigned me back to *W. W. Bushman Elementary School,* where I had spent the previous seven years as a teacher and administrative intern. Receiving this assignment was the completion of my *Ultimate Goal – to become a school principal.* After being employed for only eight years with the district, I had now been assigned to lead the second-largest elementary school in the Dallas Independent School District. The student population was a little over 1,200. What an awesome responsibility! *I ask again, do you have goals set for yourself?*

# My Journey

**W. W. BUSHMAN ELEMENTARY SCHOOL**
(July 1984-June 1988) *RETURNED AS PRINCIPAL*

    I remember being quite anxious and nervous that summer before the opening of the new school year. It was a very stressful yet exciting summer for me. It was so stressful I broke out in hives on the back of my legs and had to go to the doctor. He said it was my nerves. You see, I was extremely busy that summer because I was working on three different assignments at the same time. The principal at B. F. Darrell had just received a new assignment to open one of the newly created "Learning Centers in South Dallas" and, therefore, had to be away from Darrell a lot during the closing of the school year. That meant I had to be very instrumental in helping to close out the school year.

    Also, prior to being informed that I would be promoted to the principalship for the upcoming school year, I had already accepted a *summer school assignment* as principal of Adelle Turner Elementary School. Thus, I was preparing for that assignment as well. While all this was going on, the superintendent called me to his office and informed me that I had been promoted to the principalship and assigned to W. W. Bushman Elementary School. I certainly was not expecting this, so I had to begin SERIOUS

# My Journey

preparation for that BIG challenge. With all these assignments going on simultaneously, I am sure that is why I broke out in hives.

After I came to grips with the different challenges facing me, I settled down, prioritized the various tasks confronting me at each school, and then got busy with my planning efforts. Somewhere I read, "If you fail to plan, you plan to fail!" Therefore, I needed to prepare and present myself as a capable and confident administrator in each assignment. I didn't leave any stones unturned. As I planned for the opening of Bushman, I had to keep in mind that most of the staff members there consisted of the same people I had been teaching alongside for the past several years. Therefore, I knew without a doubt, if I was going to make a good impression in my new role as principal, then I would have to "up my game." I had to go in as prepared as possible so they would *see and respect me as the new principal and leader of this huge school.*

Looking back, I think I managed those three assignments quite well: 1) Working as a team, the principal and I successfully closed out B. F. Darrell; 2) Being blessed with an awesome summer school staff, I had a very good experience as *summer school principal* at Adelle Turner; and 3) I worked diligently to get ready for the school opening activities as principal of W. W.

# My Journey

Bushman. *Lesson Learned: You don't get a second chance to make a first impression!*

Many teachers and staff complimented me throughout the week on how impressed they were with the degree of organization and how smoothly everything was going during our first week of staff development at Bushman. Some talked about how proud they felt as "Black" teachers watching their young, Black principal conduct workshops and presentations in such a professional manner. They were excited and ready to start the upcoming school year. Both White and Black teachers expressed this type of sentiment. The letters below are just a small sample of the kind of letters of encouragement and support I received from many teachers, students, and my superintendent:

*"Dear Dr. Bell,*

*This letter is to thank whoever is responsible for hiring Mr. Lincoln Butler as principal of W. W. Bushman Elementary School. Mr. Butler, in a few short weeks, has instilled in me the fervor to do an outstanding job. To hear this man speak and express his views and expectations gives me a surge of energy. Never before at Bushman have I felt such a positive feeling. For the first time I feel*

# My Journey

*we have an administrator who can actually understand the frustrations of teachers and share in the joys. He's exciting.*

*Since my first year at Bushman, I have been impressed with Mr. Butler, the man who taught one of my sixth graders to read (yes, read-it was a tragic case). Someone had the insight to move him into administration. He is definitely a leader and a boss I am proud to work for.*

*I do hope D.I.S.D. allows Mr. Butler to remain at W. W. Bushman for a while. I believe he will surpass Mr. Don Williams' remarkable gains." Very truly yours,* **Sally Z.** *(Sept. 13, 1984)*


*"Mr. Butler,*

*I am thankful to God for sending us a leader to W. W. Bushman like you. Not only did the DISD groom you, I feel God had a part in this grooming. You are a leader from the heart. It was visible in you before you were chosen. I am very proud of you, and I know your family feels the same. I will put my Boss up against any boss because he does not have to get his act together. He stays together. God bless you Mr. Butler and may He forever keep you."*
**Mrs. Cloteal Cameron (Sis), 5<sup>th</sup> Grade Teacher** *(10/16/84)*

# My Journey

*"Dear Mr. Butler,*

*Happy Mr. Butler's Day to you! As the principal of this school, I commend you for your hard work. I know being principal of a school with over 1400 students is a big responsibility. Your love and care for us have shown throughout the entire school year. For this, I think you deserve a title, "Mr. Lincoln Butler, The Father of W. W. Bushman." Your being principal this year has really made my last year of elementary school a special treat. Thanks, Mr. Butler, for showing that you really care about me. Sincere Thanks."* **Yanna L., sixth grade student** *(May 16, 1986)*


*"Lincoln,*

*I have been very proud of my appointment of you as principal of W. W. Bushman and have observed on a regular basis, your accomplishments and the improvements that have been made at Bushman since you became principal."* **Dr. Linus Wright, Former General Superintendent** *(December 15, 1986)*

# My Journey

# MAJOR CHALLENGES FACED AS PRINCIPAL OF BUSHMAN

**STUDENT DISCIPLINE**

When I first arrived back at Bushman as principal, student discipline was an issue that had to be addressed immediately. I have always believed that providing students with opportunities to succeed and recognizing their success would boost their self-esteem. Ultimately, it would have a positive effect on their behavior. So, I talked with the teachers in grades 4-6 about recommending some misbehaving students to serve as "Safety Patrols" for the campus. Several teachers quickly rebuffed this idea and felt it would send the wrong message of rewarding students for being "disruptive."

After much discussion, I convinced the teachers to support this idea for a "trial period" of six weeks. If the idea did not work, we would make changes as needed. I then selected two very positive and progressive-thinking teachers to serve as sponsors for the safety patrols, and I asked them to develop some rules and

# My Journey

guidelines for the students to follow. I also asked them to provide incentives for the students, including occasional social activities such as an ice cream party, certificates of improvement, etc.

After the students had been selected, we provided training on how to conduct themselves while on duty. We held weekly meetings with the students to highlight their successes and to provide guidance and assistance. The students were also encouraged to share their thoughts and ask questions. I think this made them feel important because they could spend quality time in a positive, non-threatening setting with "some of their teachers and the principal!"

I often reminded the students they were representing their principal, parents, teachers, and the entire school. The kids loved participating in the program. We received positive comments from the teachers and staff commending the students for their efforts; also, notes about improvement in their classwork were received. The program proved very successful and student discipline improved as a result!

# My Journey

**NEW TEACHER APPRAISAL SYSTEM**

During the 1985-86 school year, the Dallas ISD introduced a new Teacher Appraisal System designed by Dr. Richard Manatt. This new appraisal system required the building administrator to conduct two or four *(I don't remember which)* formal observations of each teacher during the school year, and a "second appraiser" *(usually the assistant principal or other administrator)* was required to observe the **same class at the same time**.

My assistant principal left the Dallas ISD after the third week of school that year for personal reasons. The district did NOT replace her until the following spring, during the *last week of April*, so I did not have a second appraiser. Therefore, I had to contact other assistant principals and coordinate my schedule with their schedules to conduct observations simultaneously.

As I remember, after each observation, I also had to compare the reports and complete a third form that would be used during the conference with the teacher. At the end of the school year, I had to conduct my summative conferences with all the teachers and the support staff! Additionally, I still had to do everything else required of a building principal with a student

# My Journey

population of more than 1200 and nearly 80 classroom teachers with no assistant principal!

Finally, the district sent me an assistant principal on **April 26** of that spring semester. A LOT OF GOOD THAT DID ME. HECK, THE SCHOOL YEAR WAS OVER. BY THAT TIME, AND I HAD ALREADY COMPLETED ALL OF MY CLASSROOM OBSERVATIONS.

To say that this was a challenging year for me is truly an understatement! However, not only did our school survive, BUT WE THRIVED!!

*Lesson Learned: Don't complain; just buckle down and get the job done! As the late Dr. Robert Schuller once said,* **"Tough Times Never Last, But Tough People DO!"**

Someone else said, "When the going gets tough, the tough get going!"

**AND THAT IS PRECISELY WHAT WE DID!**

I faced many more challenges that year. Here are just a few:

# My Journey

- Frequent School Break-ins with many broken windows – I remember vandals broke 43 windows in our building during one weekend. This was a tough community.
- Difficult, Intrusive Individuals from the Community – This created many challenges for me, but I was NOT going to be intimidated! There were times during the summer when I worked alone at the school, and I had to take some "precautionary measures" to keep myself safe.
- High Teacher Turnover Rate – This resulted in many new and inexperienced teachers being assigned to fill vacancies.

Despite the challenges we faced at Bushman, the following are some of the highlights of our achievements while I served as principal:

- PTA Attendance Increased dramatically.
- Student Discipline improved greatly.
- Parent participation increased, and for the most part, they were very supportive.
- Student Achievement Increased.

**PRINCIPAL RECOGNITION**

# My Journey

May 16, 1986, was designated **"Lincoln Butler Day"** at W. W. Bushman Elementary School. The faculty, staff, students, and parents planned the whole day in my honor. The guests included my former supervisors:

1. **Mr. Robert Craft** - my first principal when I began teaching at W. W. Bushman in November 1976.
2. **Ms. Jacqueline Harrell** - Dean of Instruction at Bushman when I arrived as a teacher.
3. **Mr. Don Williams** - my third principal while teaching at Bushman. I was also promoted to *administrative intern* and became a member of Mr. Williams' administrative team. I learned so much from him.
4. **Ms. Louise Smith** - the principal at B. F. Darrell during the one-year I served as assistant principal. Very supportive!
5. **Dr. Frank Alexander** - my immediate supervisor while principal at Bushman.

I was extremely honored to have these outstanding administrators interrupt their busy schedules and come to Bushman to support me during this recognition program. I had previously worked for and alongside each of them and learned so much from

## My Journey

them. I will forever be grateful for their genuine support, guidance, and encouragement throughout the years I have known them!

Robert Craft    Dr. Frank Alexander    Jacqueline Harrell    Don Williams    Lincoln Butler

Private lunch in my office with Ms. Louise Smith.
I served as Ms. Smith's assistant principal for one year at B. F. Darrell before returning to Bushman as principal.

# My Journey

I served as principal of W. W. Bushman for four years (1984-1988). And while we had to deal with many adverse issues,

# My Journey

I remain incredibly proud of the accomplishments that we (administrators, teachers & staff, parents, and students) achieved.

The job of a school principal requires a strong commitment and is very demanding, especially if you are trying to do your absolute best for the children in your care. There is no way I could have successfully met these requirements without the love and support of my wife and children, to whom I will forever be grateful. I was very pleased when the Dallas Post Tribune recognized us as **"Family of the Week."**

Courtesy of the Dallas Post Tribune

After four successful years as principal of W. W. Bushman Elementary School, I was then promoted to Principal of T. W. Browne Middle School.

**T. W. BROWNE MIDDLE SCHOOL**

# My Journey

### (June 1988-June 1989)

I spent the summer planning and getting familiar with the campus and community, reviewing the student achievement data, etc. Also, during that summer, I met separately with the following groups so I could hear their views on what was needed to move the school forward:

- PTA Executive Board
- Site-Based Decision-Making Committee
- All Department Heads

During these meetings, I took notes and used this valuable, first-hand information to assist in my planning before the opening of school. By the time school opened, I was quite familiar with the needs and had begun developing relationships with some staff and community members. Because of the success of these summer

# My Journey

meetings, I started using this strategy at each subsequent school I was assigned to during my career.

When I first arrived at T. W. Browne, I noticed the teachers and staff members who smoked did so out at the front entrance of the school. When finished, they would put their cigarettes out on the front porch and go back inside. As a result, the front entry to the building stayed littered with cigarette butts. This was one practice that I addressed immediately. Also, one of the things that I learned during my summer meetings with the various groups was that several staff cars were stolen during previous years. Now, every teacher had a "duty period" where they were assigned to a particular location in the building to provide supervision and monitoring. So, when I stopped the staff from smoking at the front entrance of the building, I designated the back porch right next to the teacher parking lot as one of the areas where smoking was permitted. I also assigned this area as a "duty station." That way, there would always be someone watching the parking lot during every period of the school day. Consequently, we DID NOT have a single car stolen or tampered with that year.

*Lesson Learned, Little things make a BIG difference!*

As the school year got started, I thought about what Dr. H. B. Bell, assistant superintendent, would often remind the principals

## My Journey

new to a campus. He would advise us not to go in trying to change everything immediately. *He said we should observe and then make changes as needed.* During the first three months, I spent a great deal of time observing and taking notes. Then I called a faculty meeting to deliver my "Three Month Observation Report." I discussed a litany of Updates and Changes in Specific Building Procedures and Policies that needed immediate attention.

The following are some of the items I addressed during this meeting:

1. Teachers and staff were accustomed to leaving the campus without permission during their planning and duty periods. I informed the staff this violated district policy and must cease immediately.
2. There was a form in the office the teachers could fill out and take off early from work without speaking to or getting permission from an administrator. They would go into the office and complete the form and say, *"I gotta leave early!"* and off they went. I also stopped this practice immediately and got rid of that form. No one was permitted to leave the campus without the approval of an administrator and only for emergency purposes.
3. Brewing coffee in the classroom – I considered this to be unprofessional, and it posed a potential danger and hazard for students and the teacher. This was stopped immediately.

# My Journey

4. In-fighting and bickering among staff members. (I shared and discussed a document with them that Dr. Bell gave to his principals entitled, "Ten Commandments of How to Get Along with People."
5. Signing in and signing out. (This is the responsibility of each staff member that cannot be delegated.)
6. I also indicated that more specific "Departmental" changes would be forthcoming.

These are a few practices the staff was accustomed to before my arrival. In addition to dealing with many staff issues, we had a serious "gang" problem. *(District officials shared this with me **after** I had accepted the position.)* You see, T. W. Browne was in a nice, quiet neighborhood made up of adults whose children had grown up and, for the most part, had moved away. Therefore, much of the student body of Browne consisted of students who were **bussed in** from six different elementary school communities. We had 16 or more buses from these different communities roll in each morning. Imagine that!

As a result, we had to deal with many student disturbances, some quite serious. Usually, whatever altercations the students were involved in over the weekend in their communities would carry over to the school on Monday morning. More often than not, this resulted in fights around the school. Often, the serious

# My Journey

disturbances required us to hold official hearings with the parties involved, including the parents. This happened very frequently and was very time-consuming.

In addition to the gang problem, the students were accustomed to hanging out in the halls after the tardy bell rang and then going to class late. I decided to start having "tardy sweeps." There were three floors to the building and there were three administrators. I assigned each of us to a floor. I told the teachers to close the doors after the tardy bell rang and not allow anyone to enter their classroom until an administrator had dealt with them.

Anyone caught in the halls after the bell rang without a pass from a staff member would receive one "lick" from a paddle by the administrator assigned to that hall. They would then be allowed to enter the class. The noise from the paddle would reverberate off the walls and the students heard it in the classrooms. Well, it didn't take but two or three days and the tardy problem was history.

The teachers were amazed! I remember one coach telling me in all the years he had been at the school, he had never seen the halls completely clear after the tardy bell had rung. He said there were always large numbers of students milling around and not even worrying about getting to class on time. Sometimes, you have to take drastic measures to achieve success. **Problem Solved!**

# My Journey

Other problems I had to deal with include, but were NOT limited to, the following:

- Students set fires in the trash cans in the boys' restrooms
- A fire was set in the auditorium behind the stage *(We had to call the fire department for this one.)*
- My assistant principal did not report back to the campus after the Winter Break and did not return until the end of May. When he took the leave of absence, he said his knee was injured but later admitted to me that he was just tired. I then had to try to make do with two retired principals who were not very dependable. If one were absent on a given day, the other would get upset and not come in the next day. And so on, and so on.

I implored the school district administrators to provide me with another assistant principal because my enrollment dictated that I was to have two assistant principals. I also asked that they consider that my only assistant principal left at mid-year. *(He did not return until the last week of the school year.)* When the district officials told me they would take care of me next year, I informed them that I had to make it through *this year*. My immediate supervisor also

# My Journey

wrote letters requesting that I receive another administrator, all to no avail.

I must mention here that something similar to this had happened to me while I was principal at Bushman, and I was determined **NOT** to let this continue to happen to me. So, by late spring of that year, I had decided that I would not return to Browne that next year, even if it meant that I might have to leave the district. My position was if you continued to send me to "troubled" schools to clean up, then at least give me the manpower I needed to get the job done! Sometimes you must take a stand, and, as my baby boy says, **"Man Up!"**

The stress of all of this was beginning to weigh heavily on me. I remember one day, something happened to me after lunch. As I walked back to my office, I began to get dizzy and became very disoriented. I thought I was going to pass out and had to hold on to the wall to keep from falling. I had never felt like this before, and it was quite concerning, to say the least. After I got to my office, I closed the door without alerting anyone. Eventually, my head cleared up, and I tried to put this behind me.

Dallas ISD would not adequately staff my school as dictated by my student enrollment of 1,035. According to the district guidelines for staffing, middle schools with 1,001 students

# My Journey

would receive two assistant principals. I also observed another school with nearly **400** students less get two assistant principals.

*This helped solidify my decision not to return for the next school year.* So, I formally requested to be transferred from Browne beginning the next school year. Eventually, my request was granted, and I was reassigned.

### ADELLE TURNER ELEMENTARY SCHOOL
(July 1989-February 1992)

During my first summer as principal of Adelle Turner, one of my administrator colleagues *(who lived in the community)* shared with me that a couple of the teachers were already "setting traps" for me in an attempt to make me fail. Why? I don't have a clue. I didn't even know these people.

# My Journey

My friend said, *"I'm sharing this with you because when you're forewarned, you're fore-armed!"*

Before school began that fall, I spent a great deal of time at the school reviewing the class schedule, planning and preparing for school opening, walking the physical plant making notes of repairs needing attention, etc.

As was a customary part of my planning and preparation, I scheduled a meeting with the PTA Executive Board to get to know them before the school opening. I also met with some of the "key" dads in the school and we began making preparations to revitalize the Dads' Club.

One interesting practice that the parents at Adelle Turner were accustomed to was requesting and even demanding that their kids be placed in a particular teacher's classroom. This was a practice I was not ready for and put me at odds with several parents right from the beginning. NOTE: If you grant one parent's request, then naturally, they are going to tell their neighbors, who will then come up to the school and make the same type of requests/demands. I refused to make these changes.

I told them that the class assignments had already been completed and I would not make any changes. I was very professional and courteous with the parents, but I could not, and would not, begin my tenure by allowing the parents to walk into my office and make such demands.

There was no legitimate reason for those requests other than they *(the parents)* all preferred their children to be placed in certain teachers' classes. Certainly, you cannot assign every parent's child to a particular teacher of their choosing.

As principal, you cannot get into the habit of allowing parents to dictate what class their child will be placed in. I told the parents after school began if there was a legitimate problem in a classroom, we would work together with the teacher to hopefully resolve the problem to their satisfaction. Some of them left my office upset, but I stood firm.

**Working at my desk at Adelle Turner**

## My Journey

After school began, I worked closely with a group of men who had children enrolled in the school, and we re-started the Dads' Club. Their service to the school and me personally proved to be invaluable. They assisted in areas such as helping to supervise students in the lunchroom, reading to the children in the classrooms, chaperones for field trips, security for meetings held at night, serving as speakers for Career Day, judges for our field day activities, etc. The Dallas County Volunteer Association recognized their service to the school and community and presented them with the Group Volunteer of the Year Award.

# My Journey

Courtesy of DISD This Week

Dads' Club

During my tenure as principal of Adelle Turner, most of the challenges I faced came from the parents and getting them to understand their role in the school. Some of them acted as if *"they ran the school."* I remember the first year the teachers and I planned an evening workshop for parents to help them prepare their children for the upcoming standardized tests. The teachers worked hard and prepared packets with study material for the parents to use with their children. All parents had been adequately informed and the turnout was great!

As the workshop proceeded, one of the PTA Officers entered the building and, after seeing all the parents, confronted me in the hallway and **demanded** to know what was going on. This caught me off guard because the parents had received many notices regarding the workshop. That's why the attendance was so good.

That individual boldly asked me if I had cleared this through her! WOW! I immediately said to her, "Understand this. **I** am the principal of this school! **You** are a PTA Officer! I don't clear through you! You clear through ME!" I then told her, "When something goes wrong at this school, the superintendent is NOT

# My Journey

going to call PTA Officers. He's going to call the PRINCIPAL!" I then escorted her to my office, where we continued the conversation.

I remember a couple of the dads' club members witnessed this encounter and sat in on the meeting. They were appalled at the arrogance of the PTA Officer. After the meeting was over, they came and apologized for that individual's behavior and assured me they were going to "take over" the PTA the next year. And I am proud to say they did. With their support, we started accomplishing things for the children at Turner. And as time went on, I was able to win over that PTA Officer! In fact, at the End of Year Awards Program, she came to me and said if I ever decided to return to the secondary level, she would love to work for me. What a change of attitude! To God be the glory!

Overall, I had a very effective and supportive staff at Turner. By remaining firm, consistent, and fair in my interactions with the teachers, students, and parents, I was also able to win over those teachers who supposedly were setting traps for me. When my mom died in October 1990, twelve of my teachers drove to Brinkley, Arkansas, to attend the funeral

. The round trip from Dallas to Brinkley is over 800 miles. I had no idea they were coming. When I looked up and saw them

## My Journey

pulling up at the church, my heart filled with joy and gratitude. This gesture of love and support meant more to me than I can adequately describe here.

Adelle Turner staff members who attended my mom's funeral

In early January 1992, one of my former principal colleagues visited with me regarding an opportunity to work for the Texas Education Agency (TEA). After reading the materials he left with me, I discovered that the TEA was authorizing each of the twenty regional service centers to hire Field Service Agents to serve as liaisons between the school districts and the TEA.

## My Journey

The Service Centers in Fort Worth and Richardson both had openings for Field Service Agents. I was impressed with the job description and immediately began the process of completing the application and arranged an interview with both centers. I chose the center in Fort Worth basically for two reasons:

1) It was much less traffic driving to and from Fort Worth than it was driving to and from Richardson,

2) Fort Worth's center offered me the Program Director of Field Services position, which also meant a higher starting salary. So, I resigned from my position as principal of Adelle Turner and began working at Region XI Service Center in Fort Worth in February 1992.

Before I left Adelle Turner, the parents, teachers, and students got together and gave me a "going away celebration" that was second to none. There were many activities at the school involving the students and staff; the celebration then culminated that night at a nice establishment located downtown in the West End, where the administrators, teachers, parents, and friends

# My Journey

bestowed many gifts and tributes upon me. It was truly amazing, and I must say, very much appreciated!

**Teachers Sharing Tributes at Lombardi's Restaurant**

# My Journey

## REGION XI SERVICE CENTER, FIELD SERVICES
## (Feb. 1992-June 1994)

I accepted the Program Director of Field Services position at Region XI Service Center. In this role, I was responsible for the program's day-to-day operations. Additionally, I was assigned to several school districts in Region XI and served as the liaison between the Districts and the Texas Education Agency (TEA).

This meant that I worked directly with the superintendents to expedite any requests or concerns they had with services coming from the TEA. This also meant I had to travel to Austin periodically for training, conferences, etc. As the months passed, I found that I was beginning to have a lot of idle time on my hands. So, I began doing research and started conducting workshops and training on cultural diversity and multicultural education because there was a great need for this type of training in this region.

Many districts throughout Region XI began requesting my services shortly after I started these workshops. I was pleased I could fill this void in the region and thoroughly enjoyed providing the training. The audiences, including teachers and building staff, principals, central office staff, school board members, superintendents, students at Texas Christian University, etc., were very receptive to my training. I was constantly asked to return for

# My Journey

additional training and interaction. Attached is a partial copy of one of my brochures:

# My Journey

> **Samples of what others have said about this consultant's workshops and presentations:**
>
> ▫ Excellent presenter! Very engaging and informative. Sensitive to our needs and eager to answer questions. *S. Johnson*
>
> ▫ Wow! Mr. Butler really knows this area and was quite successful in sharing his ideas, experiences and strategies with us. I'd rate this workshop a 12 out of 10!! Thanks! *M. Dow*
>
> ▫ Excellent presentation. All teachers should attend this workshop. *P. Justice*
>
> ▫ It's great to know that there are such passionate principals in our schools! Thank you, Mr. Butler, for sharing with us your knowledge and experiences. *E. Pierce*
>
> ▫ Very profound and humorous speaker. Mr. Butler kept my attention and my curiosity alive. *G. Iker*
>
> ▫ Mr. Butler was interesting and the ideas he shared have real application to the classroom. *P. Petta*
>
> ▫ One of the best workshops I've been to, and I've been to many!
>
> ▫ Lincoln needs to know what an inspiration and resource he has been. *B. Gaskill*
>
> ▫ Very good speaker. Mr. Butler could be an inspirational speaker and make millions. Dallas is lucky to have him. *S. Murray*

While working at the service center, I also teamed up with **Dr. Cornell Thomas, Assistant Professor at Texas Christian University.** We created and co-taught a course at TCU entitled "Diversity in American Education." Twenty-two graduate students in the school of education participated. The following is an excerpt from a letter written by Dr. Thomas regarding this effort:

# My Journey

*"The tremendous success of this class, as expressed through student evaluations and by faculty, the department chair, and dean of the school, has resulted in Diversity in American Education becoming a core requirement in the school of education for most majors. This success was due to, to a great degree, the insightful planning and excellent instruction of Mr. Butler. Accolades from the dean, Douglas Simpson, to students support these statements."*

Additional excerpts from letters and notes regarding the diversity training that I conducted throughout Region XI and other parts of the state:

*"Lincoln, thank you for ensuring that our multicultural interdepartmental team does a quality job. The team met and exceeded my expectations—also, your presentation was superb!"*
**Marie M. (October 1992)**

*"Dear Mr. Butler, thank you so much for your part in helping to make our Fall Administrators Conference the success that it was. I heard nothing but positive comments from those who attended your session. I want you to know how much we at Region IV appreciate your help and hope you can come to Region IV again*

# My Journey

*soon." Sincerely,* **Mary G., Director, Educational Leadership (November 1993)**

*"Dear Lincoln, I just want to thank you so much for presenting BaFa BaFa on January 14. It was a huge success. My goal for your presentation was to establish a sense of cohesiveness and cultural awareness. Our goal was met. I realize that this was above the call of duty for you to come to Atherton, but I will always appreciate that you provided such a great experience for the faculty. Thank you so much for your support. Please know that you are always welcome at Atherton."* **Linda H., Principal (February 1994)**

*"Dear Mr. Butler, the Future Principal's Academy at TCU would not have been the same without your presence. Thank you for your time and presentation. You had lots to tell us, and you told us in a very positive and inspiring message. You're a gifted speaker, and I'm glad to have benefitted from your part in the seminar." Sincerely,* **Meta A. (August 1996)**

After two and a half years at the Service Center, and a change in leadership, I decided it was time to call the Superintendent of the Dallas ISD, Mr. Chad Woolery, and let him know I was getting homesick and was thinking about returning to

## My Journey

Dallas. He quickly said, *"That sounds like good news to me! When can we talk?"* We arranged a time to discuss what he had available for me and two weeks later, I was back in Dallas working at the central office administration headquarters.

**DALLAS ISD CENTRAL OFFICE ADMINISTRATION**

When I returned to Dallas ISD, I was given the position of Principal Planner, working with one of the associate superintendents. My office was in the Central Administration Building, and I remained in this position for one year. I think the superintendent just *created this position for me* to get me back in the district. Around mid-year, I informed the superintendent that I felt I was most effective in a school and would like to return to the principalship the next fall. He told me to let him what school assignment I wanted, and he would make it happen.

Later that spring, the superintendent called me to his office and said he knew what he had promised me, but he had a school in trouble and the Texas Education Agency was preparing to take it over. He said he could get the State to give him a year to restructure the school by making some changes, which included designating this campus as part of the newly created "Restructured Schools Initiative." He told me in no uncertain terms that this school needed

## My Journey

fixing NOW! He proceeded to tell me about the school and the challenges I would face.

Among those challenges were poor student achievement, discipline problems, low teacher morale, and a lack of parent participation. The superintendent then asked if I would accept the challenge of turning that school around and keeping the State from taking it over. I have always enjoyed a good challenge and had a good relationship with the superintendent. So, without hesitation, I told him I would accept the challenge and get the job done for him. That school was **Albert Sidney Johnston Elementary.**

**Lincoln Butler, New Principal of Albert Sidney Johnston**

**ALBERT SIDNEY JOHNSTON ELEMENTARY SCHOOL**
(July 1995-July 2002)

# My Journey

It didn't take long for the word to get out that I had accepted the principalship at Albert Sidney Johnston beginning the 1995-96 school year. Immediately, I started receiving calls from teachers and colleagues throughout the district asking me if I needed my head examined. I heard a lot of negative comments about Johnston. They kept asking me if I was sure I wanted to go there and informed me it could be the beginning of the end of my career. I assured all the naysayers that I was going to Johnston and was not afraid of the challenges. I told them to keep their eyes on us because they would read about us!

Keeping in mind the things the superintendent had shared with me regarding Johnston and the negative comments I had heard from my colleagues, I knew I did not have any time to waste. I started planning immediately. Thankfully, after I arrived at Johnston, I realized things were not nearly as bad as I had been led to believe. And there were some very strong, capable staff members still on board. So, it was not that much different than any other school I had been assigned to in the past.

**BEFORE SCHOOL BEGAN**

I spent a great deal of time that summer recruiting and hiring teachers and attending training. Due to teacher turnover,

## My Journey

teacher burnout, and teachers removed from the campus by the superintendent, I had to replace about half of the teaching staff at Johnston. While this was a daunting task late in the hiring season, it wasn't all bad because it allowed me to recruit some of the outstanding teachers I had worked with in some of my previous principal assignments. Because this campus was now in the "Restructured Schools Initiative," the superintendent made special provisions for approving the transfer of teachers who wanted to join me at Johnston. This was a significant factor in helping me get off to a GREAT start.

In addition to filling vacancies, I started reviewing past achievement history for Johnston to identify areas needing the most attention. I also wanted to see if there were any identifiable "trends" that I could pick up. This would be valuable information as I began restructuring the schedule and reassigning teachers. I also spent much time familiarizing myself with the physical school plant and the surrounding community.

In July, I scheduled separate meetings at the school with the Grade Level Chairs, the PTA Executive Board, and other "key" community members. The main purpose of the meetings was for these important individuals to have an opportunity to tell me what they felt were the reasons the school was at a point where the state

# My Journey

was preparing to take it over. I listened intently and took notes. The information I gained was invaluable and put me well "ahead of the game" with my planning and preparation for the school opening in the fall. These meetings also allowed me to share information about my leadership style and my observations and expectations for the upcoming school year.

Another important takeaway from these meetings was that they allowed me to get to know many of my teachers and the parent leadership in the school and community before the school year started. By the time the *first bell rang*, I was ready and hit the ground running!

**AFTER SCHOOL BEGAN (Setting Expectations)**

During the first week of school, we were involved in staff development activities, and I must say everything went very well. Everyone was excited and really fired up! I was so confident that we would have a fantastic week of training that I even invited some district officials and parent leaders to attend the first sessions. They were all very impressed and praised the staff for their energy, camaraderie, and teamwork. Our planning and preparation during the summer paid off.

# My Journey

I also met with each group of employees (assistant principal, professional and support staff, custodial, and lunchroom staff). During these meetings, I explained that **the evaluation process begins on the first day of school** and extends through the last day of the school year. *Many staff members assume the evaluation is just a process we must conduct at the end of the school year.*

I shared with them the summative evaluation conference is just what it says: a summation and evaluation of your entire school year, including the good and the areas needing improvement. I also provided each staff member with a copy of their duties and responsibilities for their specific position. We discussed the content and then signed the document. A copy was given to the staff member and a copy was placed in their personnel files. I shared with the staff members that my expectations were high for everyone, starting with myself. I stressed that by working together we would be able to accomplish our goals.

I am pleased to say that everyone bought into our mission and was really working together and supporting each other, *except the assistant principal,* who had been reassigned from a high school to Johnston. Over a period of a few weeks, she had managed to clash with most of the staff and was also going against my

# My Journey

directives. After a couple of one-on-one conferences with her, I realized she was not the right fit for what we had been charged to do at Johnston.

Remember, the superintendent did not mince words when he told me this school needed fixing now! We had absolutely no time to waste. I called my supervisor, explained what was going on, and requested a conference with the assistant principal and me. Because of the urgency of my request, my supervisor showed up at Johnston the next day. As soon as the conference began, the assistant principal started lying and fabricating all sorts of untrue stories about what was going on at Johnston. She told my supervisor I had screamed in her face.

After a few minutes into the conference, my supervisor said to her, *"Let me stop you right now! I do not believe for one minute the things you are saying. I KNOW LINCOLN BUTLER! And I will not sit here and listen to you tell these lies. I will move you from Johnston ASAP, and while you are waiting for your transfer, I DO NOT want Mr. Butler to give me another bad report on you. DO YOU UNDERSTAND ME?"*

Wow! You see, this was not the first time my supervisor and I had worked together. She was also my supervisor at one of my previous principal assignments, so we knew each other quite

# My Journey

well. After about a week, my supervisor transferred the assistant principal and replaced her with someone who came in and immediately got on board with us. She was very positive and supportive of the entire staff, students, and parents.

To help build a sense of *esprit de corps* throughout the campus, my outstanding music teacher, Mrs. Carolyn Wilson, came to me and informed me that we should use the song "Let's Give Them Something To Talk About" by Bonnie Raitt to inspire our staff. I thought this was a fantastic idea and this song became our "battle cry" that year. We would sing it at many of our meetings, which helped keep everyone excited and fired up. It helped build camaraderie and teamwork among the staff.

> *"Let's give them something to talk about; Let's give them*
> *something to talk about,*
> *talk about J-o-h-n-s-t-o-n!"*

(And buddy, we DID.)

On September 12, 1995, the PTA, faculty, and staff held a reception welcoming the new principal to Johnston. By the end of the first week, I had met with all the students and discussed my expectations. I encouraged each of them to learn the School Motto and Student Creed. I would challenge the students to recite them

# My Journey

from time to time, and I would hold them accountable to conduct themselves accordingly.

**SCHOOL MOTTO**
**EXCELLENCE!**
**NO LESS EXPECTED! NO LESS ACCEPTED!**

**STUDENT CREED**
**I BELIEVE IN MYSELF AND MY ABILITY TO DO MY BEST AT ALL TIMES.**
**I WILL LISTEN, SPEAK, THINK, REASON, READ, AND WRITE. I WILL DO**
**ALL OF THESE THINGS WITH ONE PURPOSE IN MIND:**
**TO DO MY BEST AND NOT WASTE THIS DAY.**

As I moved throughout the building, in and out of classes, if I noticed students not conducting themselves appropriately, I would remind them of our School Motto and Student Creed. I would then have them recite it for me *or with me*. I did this very positively, and this strategy proved to be quite useful and helped build the student's self-esteem.

By the way, the students who were on task and behaving themselves were also given opportunities to recite the motto and creed and they loved it! I worked hard to get to know and build a rapport with my students. I wanted them to see that I truly cared about them. *It is amazing how well students respond to you after you have made a positive connection with them.*

# My Journey

Throughout the school year, we implemented many effective strategies and provided different types of incentives for students, teachers, and parents to help keep the morale high and everyone motivated. We were also instrumental in getting some school adopters and mentors to partner with us to help our children and staff.

As a result of all the hard work and dedication of our teachers, parents, and school supporters, we received many awards and accolades over my seven years as principal of Johnston. See the partial list below:

- Johnston featured in the Dallas Morning News, Post Tribune, and several community papers
- Principal received the first Umoja Award for Community Service from Radio Stations V100 and Haven 97. Councilwoman Barbara Mallory Caraway presented the award
- Principal was the special guest on Radio Stations V100 and Haven 97 on three occasions
- Principal received School Improvement Award from State Representative Helen Giddings
- Principal received the "1996 Citizen of the Year" award from Omega Psi Phi Fraternity for school improvement and community service
- Johnston received monetary awards for continuing to increase student attendance rates each year

# My Journey

- "Unveiling Ceremony" - The staff at Johnston held an impressive ceremony unveiling the portrait of Principal Lincoln Butler, which was hung in the school corridor
- The Dallas Foundation recognized Johnston as a "1996 Gold Star Winner for the Dallas Public Schools' School Performance Improvement Awards"
- Johnston received the Outstanding Achievement Award from Dr. Yvonne Ewell, District 5 School Board Trustee
- Johnston received School Improvement Awards for Exceeding Performance Expectations set by the Dallas District (1996, 1997, 1998, 2000, 2001, and 2002)
- Johnston was selected as "School of the Week" by the Dallas Post Tribune
- Johnston received much media coverage (TV, Radio, and Newspapers) regarding many of the exciting things that happened over the seven years that I was principal)
- One of Johnston's students was the Grand Prize Winner of the Emmitt Smith Reading Contest and received a $77,000 Full Paid Scholarship to the University of Dallas
- Two of Johnston's students were awarded college scholarships for winning the Second Annual Dr. Frederick Todd Chess Classic Tournament
- Johnston's GTE Saturday Scholar Program received a full-page feature article in the Dallas Public School "District Times"
- The Omega Psi Phi Fraternity, Theta Alpha Chapter, was featured on Channel 8's Metro Program for volunteer service in Johnston's Saturday Scholar Program

# My Journey

- Clarice Tinsley featured the Omega Psi Phi Fraternity on Channel 4 for their volunteer work at Johnston
- Clarice Tinsley (Channel 4) also featured a group of "Retired Omega Men as her "Hometown Heroes" for Volunteering and Mentoring a group of boys at Johnston
- Principal recognized as the "1998 Outstanding Elementary Educator of the Year by the Oak Cliff Chamber of Commerce."
- Lincoln Butler named "Principal of the Year for Area 5 – 2001
- Butler's Reading Well Dedication Ceremony – In Honor of Principal Lincoln Butler, February 1998
- The Seattle, Washington School District selected the Principal and two teachers during January 23-26, 2001, to conduct workshops at the Principals' Leadership Institute. Conference attendees included the campus administrators, central office administrators, and campus leadership teams. The conference's theme was "Eliminating Disproportionality: Closing The Achievement Gap." Johnston's presentations focused on: "Turning Around A Low-Performing School"; and "Providing Safety-Nets for Children: Strategies and Initiatives That Work"

Based on the evaluations and direct feedback, Johnston's Team was hugely successful. As a result of the effectiveness of these workshops, the superintendent of the Seattle School District

## My Journey

sent a driver to pick me up from my hotel and had me brought to his office.

He offered me a job right on the spot! He had already done some research and informed me that he also knew my wife worked for Delta Airlines and he would take care of her too. I told him I would have to think about it, but after I returned home, I declined the offer and chose to stay in Dallas.

The Johnston Team relaxing before the conference began:
**Chandra Cooper, Carolyn Wilson, Lincoln Butler**
**(Seattle, Washington)**

Without describing all the specific strategies we implemented at Johnston, I think we were very, very successful. Our superintendent got his wish: *We turned Johnston around and saved it from being taken over by the state.* At the end of my first year at Johnston, the Department of Institutional Research

# My Journey

evaluated our progress and wrote the following in its evaluation summary, "Albert Sidney Johnston has moved from being named one of the *least effective* to being recognized as one of the **most effective K-6 schools in Dallas**."

The following are letters of commendation from my school board member and my immediate supervisor:

*"Dear Lincoln,*

*Let me begin by commending you for the outstanding administrator that you are. Congratulations on the metamorphosis that has taken place at Johnston and the unusual involvement of the community, particularly the men. The Albert Sidney Johnston community should be justly proud!*

*I am exceptionally pleased with the reforms being implemented at Johnston. Your accomplishments underscore the fact that qualitative change in schools is possible.*

*Again, I commend you on your extraordinary leadership."*

**Sincerely, Yvonne Ewell, School Board Member – District 5 (May 31, 1996)**

*"Dear Mr. Butler,*

*Thank you for inviting me to your "pre-school" orientation with your staff. It was wonderful to see how enthusiastic and*

## My Journey

*positive they all are. Of course, it's easy to see why they are so energetic and of good spirit. They know they are fortunate to be at a school that is truly being reformed and revitalized by a gifted leader. It's a pleasure to work with you and Johnston school. I look forward to even greater things to be accomplished by Albert Sidney Johnston School this year."* **Sincerely, Mary Roberts, Assistant Superintendent, Cluster – 4 (Aug. 10, 1996)**

Shown here are a few additional supporting documents:

**Principal of the Year - Area 5, Spring 2001**

Principals from Areas 4, 5, and 6 were *For Principals Only* honorees in the second quarter. The winners are (left to right, with plaques) Lincoln Butler, Albert Sidney Johnston Elementary School; Sylvia Lopez, Raúl Quintanilla Sr. Middle School; and Robert E. Craft, W.H. Atwell Fundamental Academy. They are flanked by representatives of MetLife Resources, event sponsor.

Courtesy of the Dallas ISD

# My Journey

*We share a unique connection: Mr. Robert Craft was my principal when I was a teacher at W. W. Bushman; Ms. Sylvia Lopez was my counselor when I was principal at W. W. Bushman. We have all been selected as Principal of the Year for our respective Areas! Pretty cool!*

**Butler's Reading Well**

# My Journey

*This was dedicated in my honor by the staff – February 1998.*

Lincoln Butler, Dr. Yvonne Ewell, Dr. Robert Cooter

# My Journey

### Portrait "Unveiling"

Presented by the Oak Cliff Chamber of Commerce – May 1998

# My Journey

Let me spend some time here discussing why I retired from the Dallas Independent School District at age fifty-four. I certainly did not want to retire so young, but as I mentioned in an earlier chapter, I had been dealing with severe migraine headaches for most of my life. However, I pushed through each day because I knew I had to work.

After I was assigned to Johnston, I began spending almost every day at the campus that summer involved in planning and meeting with teachers, parents, community members, and others. The bottom line, I was spending a lot of time on the campus. Sometime around September or October, I realized I constantly had to clear my throat with a little cough. This was not normal. Also, I noticed if I drank cold water, I would start coughing immediately. This was also unusual.

As time went on, this condition got much worse. So much so that I had to go to the doctor. I was told I had developed a sinus infection. Now, I had never had a problem with sinuses in my life before going to Johnston. By late spring of my first year at Johnston, I started coughing one night at home and lost consciousness.

My wife became alarmed at my unusual coughing and heard a loud thud. When she ran to see what had happened, she

# My Journey

found me on the floor in the hallway, not breathing, and my eyes were open. She thought I had died and was getting ready to call 911. But by the grace of God, after a moment or two, my wife said I started breathing again.

During the rest of the summer, I did okay. But as soon as school began in the fall of my second year at Johnston, the coughing returned and worsened over time. It became so severe that I had surgery in February 1997, the first of **FOUR** over time. The reason for these surgeries was my sinus cavities would become blocked with polyps. When I would cough three or four times I couldn't get any air back into my lungs, and consequently, I would pass out. The weekend before my first surgery, I was unconscious **"16 times"** and had *never* been unconscious before this all started!

Without a doubt, I knew something in that building was causing me to experience these problems. I shared this with my supervisor and the school district's doctor, and this prompted the Dallas ISD to order an Air Quality study at the campus. Each staff member and regular subs were asked to complete a survey, and when the results came back, it was discovered that ***every teacher and the subs began experiencing sinus problems AFTER they started working at Johnston***. The findings from the Air Quality study indicated there were indeed some adverse things found, but

# My Journey

it was reported that there was not a heavy enough concentration of anything in particular to cause the problems I was experiencing. **I didn't believe it then, nor do I believe it NOW!**

I know for a fact there was something in that building causing my problems and nearly destroyed my career and my life! My career was cut short because of my medical issues, which cost me greatly financially, emotionally, and health-wise. I theorized that my problem was much more severe than any of the other staff members because I spent much more time in the building than they did. It should be noted that I had previously worked at several other campuses in Dallas and three other states before coming to Texas, and I had never experienced any respiratory problem, EVER!

I ended up having to take an "early retirement," and this certainly cost me financially because I would like to have worked another ten years or so. In addition to the financial loss, I am still dealing with health challenges I will have to endure for the rest of my life.

Because of the four sinus surgeries, the tear duct in my right eye was closed entirely, and whenever that eye watered, the tears would just run down my face. Everyone thought I was crying all the time. As a result of this condition, I had surgery, and a tube was

# My Journey

placed in the right tear duct so the water would drain through my nostril and not run down my face.

Next, because of all the coughing, I developed bronchitis and eventually lost much of my hearing in both ears. Therefore, in April 2012, I had tubes put in both ears so I could hear properly again. Additionally, due to the effects of all the surgeries, I lost my sense of *smell* and much of my sense of *taste*. As a result of all the complications related to the sinus issues I developed while working at Johnston, I have had to take many medications and endure a lot of pain and discomfort.

The severity of my sinus problems, and all the other medical conditions I experienced because of the sinus issues, coupled with the migraines I had dealt with since I was a young boy, became too much. My doctors advised getting away from so much stress. One of my doctors told me because of the problems I was experiencing, if I did not get from under the stress, it was going to kill me.

So, after seven successful years as principal of Albert Sidney Johnston, I took my doctor's advice and retired. However, this was NOT something I wanted to do at such a young age. I was only fifty-four. Even now in 2023, I am still dealing with the

# My Journey

residual effects of the problems I developed while working at Johnston.

I frequently get ear infections; I am not allowed to get water in my ears; I still have coughing spells that sometimes get to the point where I am close to losing consciousness *(I have medication that I take when this occurs.)*; I still get sinus infections; I never got my sense of smell back, and my sense of taste is still not up to par, etc.

NOTE: Years after this all began, I talked with an attorney but the time to file a claim had passed. You have a "two-year window" to file this type of claim.

*When this all began happening back in 1995, I had no idea this was a condition that would **affect me the way it has and stay with me throughout the rest of my life!** So, how would I know to file a claim within two years? Plus, that was not my intention when this began.*

Let me make something clear, I don't want this to sound like a "pity party." To the contrary. I am only trying to clarify why I retired so young. I will forever be grateful to God for allowing me to work as long as I did before I had to take the early retirement.

## My Journey

He then provided me with a "part-time" job so that I could continue working on my own schedule, while doing something I thoroughly enjoyed, mentoring teachers and assisting them with their certification requirements. So, through it all, I am very appreciative and feel richly blessed. God is GOOD!

**I retired from the Dallas Independent School District in June 2002.**

# My Journey

# Retirement Reception – June 2002

My granddaughter, Teneisha, and Snow at the Retirement Reception

1995  **Lincoln Butler**  2002
**Principal**
**Albert Sidney Johnston Elementary**

**Giving my "Farewell Speech" at the Retirement Reception!**

# My Journey

## MCGRAW-HILL PUBLISHING COMPANY
### (July 2002-June 2003)

Immediately after retiring from the Dallas ISD, I was approached by representatives from two textbook publishing companies about working for them part-time as a consultant. I decided to go with McGraw-Hill, and they quickly flew me to New York City to visit and tour the main headquarters. They even had a driver pick me up at the airport and take me to my hotel. NOT BAD!

During the first half of the year, I stayed busy and traveled. However, things began to slow down around January or February, and I became very bored.

My wife and I went on vacation during the early part of July and when we returned home, I had a message from the Superintendent of Cedar Hill ISD indicating he would like to speak with me and asked me to give him a call.

Snow looked at me and said, "What does he want to talk to you about?" I told her I was not sure, but it was probably related to a job. I then told her I was retired and NOT looking for a job. Well, that's what I thought!

# My Journey

## CEDAR HILL HIGH SCHOOL (July 2003-July 2005)

After returning the superintendent's call, he invited me to come and meet with him regarding the possibility of becoming the high school principal. Now, I had been offered high school principalships while I worked in the Dallas ISD but refused to accept them because I was getting close to retirement and did not think it would be wise to take on a challenge that big. I was also concerned about all the health challenges I had been enduring for years and felt that working at the high school level would only exacerbate my problems.

But I kept my appointment, went to Cedar Hill, and met with the superintendent, Dr. Jim Gibson. He was very polite and made me feel very comfortable. We talked at length about my

# My Journey

experiences and his goals and expectations for his district. He was also honest with me about the student's behavior at the high school. He told me they were totally out of control. *(I spoke with the outgoing principal, who indicated there were major fights every week.)*

I shared with Dr. Gibson that I had previously turned down the principalship at the high school level in Dallas because I was getting close to retirement and did not think it was in my best interest. He indicated that he had other principal positions in the district and I could select whichever I wanted.

He said he just wanted me in his District. But he kept pushing me to take high school. He shared with me all the reasons he thought I would be successful at the high school. He was very convincing and asked me if I would be willing to come back and meet with his interview panel before ruling it out. I agreed.

When I returned to the district headquarters for the formal interview, there were four or five individuals on the interview team, two of whom were students from the high school. The interview went very well, and the superintendent offered me the job. I told him I needed to discuss it with my wife and my sons.

The students were very impressed and strongly encouraged me to accept the position. I was not sure I wanted to come out of

# My Journey

retirement and accept a principalship at the high school level, especially one that was out of control with a student population of more than **2,400** in grades 9-12.

After about a week of talking to colleagues who were high school principals, I spent a great deal of quiet time thinking about how much I would have to give up if I accepted this position. I also prayed about this new job offer and talked it over with my wife and sons. Finally, I woke up one morning and told my wife I would accept the job in Cedar Hill.

She asked me if I was going to accept the position at the intermediate school. I said no, I am going to accept the high school position. She immediately said, *"I think you have lost your mind!"* I told her how much I had prayed about it and felt very calm about my decision. My health had also improved since I retired from the Dallas I.S.D. So, I called the superintendent and told him I would accept the position at the high school. He was elated and wanted me to start immediately.

Before school began, I met with each of my four assistant principals individually and then as a group. Let me add that three assistant principals had already been at the high school for a few years, and each applied for the principal's job. Since they did not get the job, I am not sure they wanted me to succeed. Several White

## My Journey

parents from the community would call me periodically and warn me to watch my back because, in their words, *"Those assistant principals are trying to destroy you in the school and community."*

My fourth assistant principal, Patrick Nash, was an energetic young man whom I brought with me. I already knew him because he was a friend of one of my sons. He was an extremely hard-working administrator and I could always depend on him. We had each other's back!

As I was planning for the school opening, I told my administrators we would be holding student assemblies during the first week of school to discuss my expectations. The response from the three ladies was we don't have student assemblies here at the high school. When I asked why not, I was told the students would turn the assembly out. I quickly asked, "Who's running the school, the students or the adults?"

I informed them we were indeed going to have student assemblies. I guaranteed them the students would not turn MY assembly out! I then met with the teachers, discussed my plan, and told them I wanted each of them to talk with their students about their conduct before the assembly. I required each teacher to sit WITH their class during the assemblies. I told the teachers I would

## My Journey

be holding them accountable for helping to keep their students under control.

Well, the first day of school for the students finally arrived, and boy, was I in for an awakening. My assistant principals and I were each at our "duty posts," waiting for the buses to arrive. As the students began to unload, I had never seen so many puffed-up faces and angry looks on the faces of students, especially on the first day of school. I later learned the students tried to look "hard" so other students would be less likely to *"mess with them."*

On the second day of school, before holding the assemblies, a BIG fight broke out in the lunchroom between two girls. Now, I have always been the type of person who will jump right in the middle of students fighting and break up the fight. So, when these girls began fighting, I ran over to break them up and at about that time, they fell to the floor. I jumped down on the floor with them and somehow managed to separate and hold them apart until one of my police officers got there to assist me. He grabbed one of the girls and I held the other until the second officer arrived.

After I got up from the floor and straightened out my clothes, I noticed how the students were staring at me. Then I heard someone whisper, **"Man, I didn't know the new principal had it like that!"** At that point, I did my best to look tough and unfazed

# My Journey

by that ordeal as I walked out of the lunchroom. But boy, after I was out of their sight, I realized how exhausted that incident had left me! But I couldn't let the students know I was out of breath.

I wanted them to know whenever trouble broke out, I would intervene! One of my police officers came to me later and told me that he admired my strength and courage, but he preferred I leave that kind of action to them because, as he said, "You're going to get hurt!" I told him I understood what he was saying, but that is just who I am. I cannot stand by and watch kids beat each other's brains out and not intervene.

We had our assemblies later that week, and I discussed my expectations with the students. I must praise my students because they behaved extremely well in the assemblies. Not a single student had to be removed! *(Two boys did, however, begin to argue in the halls after one of the assemblies but one of my little girls quickly took care of that. She got right in their faces and reminded them of what I had just talked about and told them to GET THEIR BUTTS TO CLASS, and off they went.* You go girl!*)* Let me share the contents of a few emails I got from some teachers and the student council president after the assemblies:

*"Mr. Butler, I wanted you to know that I thought the assembly today was great! Sitting with our class was a great idea!*

# My Journey

*You have a wonderful presence with the students, and you were very clear on our expectations. It was one of the best assemblies we have ever had here at CHHS!!! The Dads' Club is a great idea too!!! BRAVO!!!!!!"* **Julie W., August 19, 2003**

*"Mr. Butler, I'm so glad you're here. I've already seen a marked improvement in student attitude. They seem calmer because of all the attention they are getting. I've never heard so many "good mornings" and "yes ma'ams" in my career. Consistent structure seems to be the key. The Dads' Club is great too!"* **Kelley B., August 20, 2003**

*"Mr. Butler, thank you for the fabulous assembly yesterday. This is my seventh year in the district, and I've never attended an event where students behaved themselves so well. I want you to know I'm excited about the changes I'm seeing here. It makes me proud to be a part of this district."* **Beth S., August 20, 2003**

*"Thought the assembly went great — we appreciate you!"* **Jane T., August 21, 2003**

*"Just wanted to say great job with the Dads' Club." I had a little discipline problem today and almost immediately one of our*

# My Journey

*dads was there to talk with him and help me out. I am so excited about this new program! Thank you."* **Michelle W., August 19, 2003**

*"Mr. Butler, I have been waiting ten years for my building principal and the school district to say the things you said in the assembly this AM and mean them. I appreciate you so much. Thanks for all you do."* **Linda M., September 9, 2004**

*"Mr. Butler, I just want to tell you how much I appreciate your hard work as our new principal. Your enthusiasm has definitely been received well by the teachers and all that I have heard about you is great so far. I know you are a man of strong convictions and I'm so glad to have someone like you at our school. Thank you again for everything you've already done for us and that I know you will continue to do! You are an excellent principal and a wonderful human being!"* **Melissa G., Senior Class President, August 19, 2003 \*\*Melissa was also on my interview team.**

It took a lot of hard work and perseverance to get the students' behavior under control that year. But we did NOT give up, nor did we back down. As a result, we had great success in managing our students. But, during the spring semester of my first

# My Journey

year, my sinus problems returned, and I had surgery again and was away from the campus for about three weeks. Because of these health issues, I thought about leaving after the first year, but I could not bring myself to do it because I enjoyed my job, even though it was a lot of work, and it was beginning to affect my health again.

During my second year, my sinus problems and headaches continued, and my doctor began telling me again that if I did not leave the job and get from under the stress, it was going to kill me. So, just before the Winter Break, I informed the superintendent that my health issues had caught up with me and I would have to retire again at the end of the school year. He initially tried to convince me to stay for one more year, but I told him while I did not want to leave the district, I had to listen to my body and my doctor. He understood and accepted my decision to leave.

The superintendent asked me to call a faculty meeting and inform the staff that I would retire for health reasons at the end of the school year. As I said earlier, I was not ready to leave CHHS. In fact, I had grown to love this job probably more than any of my previous principal assignments. With high school students, once you connect with them and let them know you really care about them and that you are fair, they will work hard at trying to please you and follow your directives for the most part.

# My Journey

I remember the day I met with the staff to inform them about my decision. It was a very emotional morning for me. I assembled my administrative team in my conference room and broke the news to them first. In that meeting, I teared up a little and became more and more emotional. Now, it was time to meet with the faculty and staff. As they assembled, I could feel the emotions building up inside me. I kept saying to myself, "You can do this!" Then I began to speak and completely lost it. I mean, I started crying uncontrollably. I remember one of my clerical assistants came down front and embraced me until I regained my composure. To say I felt embarrassed then, and even now, is an understatement! But my feelings were real, and I think everyone in the auditorium knew it.

I guess it got to me because I was NOT ready to leave; I knew I had not completed the work I had come there to do. But my medical conditions were taking too much of a toll on me. I remember the week before my second surgery, I could not breathe through my nostrils at all. They were completely stopped up with polys. For an entire week, I had to breathe through my mouth, including while I slept. It was horrible! And my lips became very chapped and were peeling badly.

# My Journey

Below are excerpts from letters and cards I received while preparing to leave Cedar Hill High School and notes related to our graduation ceremony:

*"Mr. Butler, I just wanted to thank you for everything you have done to help us here. You have done an excellent job. You are an excellent people person, friendly, professional, and sincere. Our school has really improved with you here. I appreciate your telling us the information you did in the meeting. Your health is important. I do hope you will be able to be here part-time if that works out."* Thanks again. **Carolyn R. (Teacher)**

*"Mr. Butler, I support you in what your decision is, but I do so with a saddened heart. I think you are a great man."*

**Coach Richard L.**

*"Mr. Butler, you will be missed. I had aspirations that you would remain until my son gets out of here. But I guess there are 1500 or more other parents with the same wish. Good luck and better health."*

**Edgar L. (Parent)**

# My Journey

*"Dear Mr. Butler, I want you to know that I have the greatest respect for you and that I will miss you and your leadership very much. I think you have been the single greatest factor in turning things around in this school since you have been here. Thank you very much for your patience."*

**Linnell R. (Teacher Assistant)**

*"Dear Mr. Butler, my name is Lawrence Stokes, I am the father of Jesse Stokes who graduated Tuesday evening. The reason for this communication is to express my heartfelt thanks for a job well done. I had an older son graduate in '03, so I have been associated with the school for the past 5 years. I can tell you this, since you arrived, I have not had to come up to the school to battle assistant principals or teachers since your arrival. Everything was handled at such a level that didn't require my presence at the school, and for that I again want to say thank you. I attended the Baccalaureate ceremony, and I was happy to hear that you're returning to Cedar Hill for another school year.*

*Although I don't have any more children attending Cedar Hill schools, I think all children will have a much better high school experience with you at the helm. Once again, I would like*

# My Journey

*to congratulate you on turning that school around. Many Blessings."*

**Lawrence S. (Parent)**

*"Mr. Butler, I would like to tell you what an awesome job you did at graduation last night. I fully expected a mess and was pleasantly surprised. The seniors were wonderful. You have done a super job."*

**Linda H., Teacher - May 26, 2004**

*"Lincoln, it is always good to visit with you. Your commitment is so evident. Thanks for all you are doing. You have to feel that you made a difference. I know that you have. I appreciate the way you are helping to manage the anxiety about who will follow you. Thanks."*

**Jim (Superintendent of Schools)**

*"Dear Mr. Butler, I write this letter to you in my absence to thank you for spending the last 2 years nurturing and loving the students at Cedar Hill High School. Your presence made a difference in more lives than you will ever know. Your quite spirit and gentleness is hard to find and it will never be forgotten. As a*

# My Journey

*parent, I have no complaints. You are special and I hope you enjoy your retirement (for the 2$^{nd}$ time). Finally, your work will not go in vain and you will be remembered in years to come."*

Love,

**Dr. D. G. Edwards, Parent - May 23, 2005**

## MORE TRIBUTES

*Hey Mr. Butler,*

*This is me, Cody Knott. I just wanted to say thank you from the bottom of my heart for everything you have done for me and for CHHS. You really have made an impact on my life. Since you became principal, I've looked up to you. You are a great leader and know how to handle things. It has really been a true pleasure to have you as our principal. I know there have been some rough spots, but I know that you worked through them and got us to where we all are now. You have helped to make our school safer and a better learning environment. You are a role model principal. It has been a great two-year journey with you. I hope the Lord blesses you and keeps you safe. I hope you are able to work with children for as long as you like. It has been an honor and a privilege to call you, my principal. You have always said "Hi" to me and asked me about things and I thank you for that. You are one of the people*

# My Journey

*from high school I'll never forget. Thank you so much and God Bless you on the rest of your journey!! Thanks for everything!"*

**Cody K., Senior, Class of 2005, February 24, 2005**

*"Mr. Butler, I am very sorry to hear that you are leaving. I have really enjoyed working with you, and hope that wherever you go that good things will follow."*

**Vickie R., Teacher, February 16, 2005**

*"Mr. Butler, I heard that you were leaving, and I just want to let you know that you will definitely be missed. My daughter, Astyne Reed, thinks very highly of you and I hope and pray that the next principal over there will be half as good with the kids as you have been. She has told me that you take time with the kids and speak to them in the hallways or wherever you see them and that has meant a lot to her. It has truly been a blessing to have you over there trying to get the high school in decent order. May God's blessings be upon you and yours."*

**Debra R., Parent, Feb. 23, 2005**

# My Journey

## THIS WORLD NEEDS MORE PEOPLE LIKE YOU
### *(Title of Card from Jessica E.)*

*"Mr. Butler, I must say that in my 16 years of living, I have never met anyone like you. I just want to say that you made a difference in my life. I appreciate you coming out of retirement to be the principal at Cedar Hill for two years. Thank you for every nomination and recommendation letter!! Thanks again."*

**Jessica E., Class of 2005, Cedar Hill High School**
**\*\*Jessica is now a celebrated and accomplished medical doctor.**

Prior to the end of the semester of my last year at Cedar Hill High School, I contacted the Director of the Education Careers Alternative Program (ECAP), Sharon Fikes. I asked her about working part-time in her program after I retired from Cedar Hill High School. *(I had conducted many workshops for Sharon and the service center when we were both employed at the Region XI Service Center in Fort Worth.)* She immediately assured me she would have a position waiting for me after I left Cedar Hill. That was good news because I was not ready to stop working completely.

# My Journey

## EDUCATION CAREERS ALTERNATIVE PROGRAM (ECAP) (August 2005-June 2021)

My employment as a Field Advisor (supervisor) with ECAP began in the fall of 2005 and continued until the summer of 2021. It is hard to believe, but I worked "part-time" with ECAP for sixteen years as a Field Advisor and truly enjoyed the experience of working with teachers in that capacity. Field Advisors are educators with several years of experience in classrooms and administrative positions. The outstanding work of field advisors is a major contribution to the success of the ECAP program.

Being employed in this capacity for 16 years gave me the opportunity to provide technical and instructional assistance to many new teachers in several school districts as they worked to obtain their teaching certification. This position also allowed me to work part-time and set my own schedule, which meant my work was basically stress-free. Thank you, Sharon, for allowing me to continue working until I was ready to *"hang it up for good!"*

# My Journey

# My Journey

## Chapter XIII: Community/Volunteer Service

*"Success has nothing to do with what you gain in life or accomplish for yourself. It's what you do for others."* Danny Thomas

*"Life's persistent and most urgent question is, what are you doing for others?"* Dr. Martin Luther King, Jr.

Dating back to my elementary school days, I have always had the propensity to want to help others. Earlier in this autobiography, I mentioned that my sixth-grade teacher had the class write about our philosophy of education. I remembered how much my teachers had helped me, so I wrote that I wanted to become a teacher to help others.

# My Journey

I don't know how to explain it, but I get such joy and fulfillment when I can help someone in need. It does not always have to be monetary. There are many other ways to position yourself to provide assistance and encouragement to others. It has been said, "To whom much is given, much is required." I sincerely believe this and try to live my life accordingly. Below, I would like to share some of the organizations where I have provided volunteer service while giving back to the community:

- **Brinkley, AR - Back to School Rally**
- *(School Supply Giveaway)*

This began in 2010 when I was asked to serve as the Emcee for the "Ribbon Cutting & Dedication Celebration" for the Marian Anderson High School Community Center of Excellence Grand Opening. While I was in Brinkley that weekend, I inquired about the possibility of providing school supplies for the students in the community. To my surprise, the community center leaders were already planning a Back-to-School Rally to give out school supplies. I told them to count me in and I would be back with school supplies and help with the rally. I returned with lots of school supplies, as I had told them I would do.

# My Journey

I was asked to give a pep talk on the day of the rally. I remember giving a brief address on the topic, *"Where one begins does not have to determine where one ends up. Your origins and background do not limit your potential."* I shared with them that I grew up in Brinkley and attended Marian Anderson High School. And while our resources were limited, I still managed to become a teacher and, ultimately, a principal at all levels. This first rally was a success and I continued to return to Brinkley with loads of supplies for the next ten years. I was also asked to give a pep talk each year thereafter. See notes and photos:

"Mr. Butler,

*Please accept my humble "thank you" for helping to make beautiful history in the City of Brinkley during the Marian Anderson High School Commission's ribbon cutting and dedication of the Marian Anderson High School Community Center of Excellence. Thank you for your travel to our town (and your town) to share the memories of yesteryear. And may God provide unto you and Mrs. Butler a special blessing for sacrificing so much to come and celebrate with us."*

**Fairy A., Founder, Marian Anderson High School Commission, Inc., July 26, 2010**

# My Journey

## \Letter of "Thanks" To My Siblings for Helping Purchase School Supplies for Brinkley

*Monday, August 9, 2010*

*Hello My Brothers and Sisters,*

*Attached you will find a copy of the supplies that Snow and I will be presenting to the Marian Anderson H. S. Community Center of Excellence for some very needy school children in Brinkley. We will drive to Brinkley this Thursday and participate in the "Back To School Rally" on Friday. The donations will be presented from "The Butler Family."*

*I sincerely appreciate each of you for helping with this most worthy project. Since I visited Brinkley this past summer, I have felt the presence of God directing my desire for our family to get involved with Brinkley and do all we can to help the children in that community. You have truly answered the call and I thank each of you. Be Blessed.*

*Lincoln*

# My Journey

## Back To School Rally – My Pep Talk to the Students and Parents

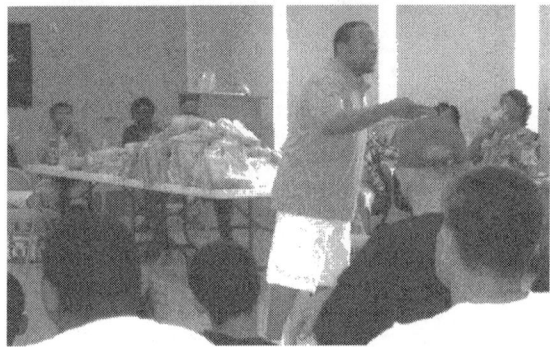

# My Journey

## Children Receiving School Supplies

*"Hello Lincoln,*

*Hope you are doing well. Thank you so much for all that you do. You and your family are a great blessing to the community center. May the Lord keep you and yours in perfect peace. Love Ya."*

**Cathy, January 29, 2014**

> **Oak Cliff Bible Fellowship (Highlights)**

I have served in several volunteer positions with our church over the years. I was a member of the following:

- Media Ministry and worked in the "Lighting Department."
- Chair of the Evaluation Committee *(A Seven-Member Committee)* for Fellowship Christian Academy.

# My Journey

Our task: conduct a comprehensive evaluation of the school and the administration. After the evaluation process was completed, an Executive Summary with Recommendations was given to the Senior Pastor of Oak Cliff Bible Fellowship – in May 2006.
- Served as a Small Group Leader for Bible Study

➢ **Omega Psi Phi Fraternity, Inc.** *(Highlights of Chapter Activity)*
- Initiated on May 9, 1993, Theta Alpha Chapter, Dallas
- Committees Served on: Annual Labor Day Picnic, Pancake Breakfast, Saturday Scholar Program, Scholarship Committee, etc.
- Scholarship Raffle – Sold the Most Tickets Within the Chapter – 405 Tickets Sold

- Life Membership, Omega Psi Phi, Fraternity, Inc.
- Saturday Scholar Program
- Citizen of the Year Award - 1996

# My Journey

➢ **African American Education Archives and History Program (AAEAHP)**
- 1st Vice President
- Chair – Oral History Committee
- Chair – Orientation Committee
- Program Manager – Digital Interactive Wall Project
- Serve on Numerous Other Committees

# My Journey

## Chapter XIV: It's Q & A Time

1. Who influenced your personal development?
    *My Mother, My Teacher-Mrs. Bryant, My Wife, My Children, and my granddaughter (Teneisha). I didn't want to disappoint them. I wanted each of them to be proud of me.*

2. What famous quote can describe your life?
    *"Where one begins does not have to determine where one ends up. Your origins and background do not limit your potential." Dr. Israel Tribble*

3. What adjectives can be used to describe you as a person?
    *Energetic, caring, hard-working, friendly, determined, family oriented.*

4. What main achievements in life are you most proud of?
    *Being married to my wife for 56 years (December 18, 1966; being the father of three dynamic, smart, and intelligent sons; being Papa to some awesome grandchildren; graduating from college; and promotion to the principalship.*

# My Journey

7. What was the most memorable and special day in your life?
   *The most memorable and special day in my life was when I married my love: Ms. Dorothy Snow Hearns. Nothing before nor since has brought me that much pride and joy. She was the most beautiful woman I had ever seen in my life, and to think, she married me. I am a blessed man, and evidently, I have favor with the Lord.*

8. What kind of hardships or tragedies did your family experience while you were growing up?
   *We were poor, but we could have done much better financially if my father had used his money more wisely.*

9. Are there any unusual genetic traits that run in your family line?
   *Several of my siblings and I have had to deal with headaches and back problems.*

10. What were *some* of your more memorable vacations?
    *Hawaii, Aruba, Grand Canyon, Cancun, San Francisco, Myrtle Beach, and East Coast (New York City, New Jersey, Philadelphia with our granddaughter, Teneisha)*

11. How would you describe your personality?
    *Somewhat relaxed and easy-going; focused; friendly; treats everyone with dignity and respect; loyal; hard-working; kind and caring.*

12. Have you ever had pets?
    *One of my co-workers gave me an awesome little Lhaso Apso dog in 1993 or '94. I named him Prince because he was such a royal-looking dog. I remember my sons getting on me because they said I would not let them have*

# My Journey

*a dog and that I waited until they left home to get one. Prince was also very protective of Snow.*

**My dog, Prince**

**Prince & Me**

13. How did you spend your summers after high school?

# My Journey

*I lived in Flint, Michigan, for the first two summers after high school. After I got married, I began spending my summers in New York City (The Bronx)*

14. If a newspaper wanted to do a story about you, what would the story be about?

    *The story would be about the sacrifices I made to take care of my family. It is whispered among some family members that I am cheap. It doesn't bother me because I have always been careful about spending my money. The reason being I never really made that much money. Teachers are some of the lowest-paid "professionals," so I had to learn how to budget. I knew I had to provide for my family, and NOTHING would come before them! As a result of being frugal with my money, whenever a sibling or friend needed help financially, I usually have been there to help. My mother taught me, **"It's not how much you manage to make; it's how you manage what you make!"***

15. Who were some of the major INFLUENCERS in your academic life?
    - *My Mom and Dad*
    - *Mrs. Bennie Bryant, Elementary Teacher and Church Member*
    - *Mr. Henry May, Supervisor-Youth Tutoring Youth, Bronx, New York*
    - *Dr. Yvonne A. Ewell, Associate Superintendent, Dallas ISD*

16. What are some of the most enjoyable times of your life?

    *Family Gatherings – Some of my life's most enjoyable and memorable times were when I got together with my brothers and sisters at one of our homes. We would eat, play cards (bring your quarters), tell big stories, laugh, and simply "hang out" together as a family. Mama raised*

# My Journey

*us to love each other, NO MATTER WHAT! I am so glad that her influence still guides us.*

17. What are some of the life lessons that you would like to pass on to your posterity?
    - *Work hard, be resilient and learn to bounce back from adversity.*
    - *Never give up.*
    - *Learn to Persevere – "Perseverance is the quality that allows you to live in such a spirit that NOTHING ever keeps you down." (Dr. Robert Schuller)*
    - *Develop a "spirit of giving." It gives you such a great sense of pride, joy, and fulfillment.*

18. What are some of the personal values that are very important to you?
    - *Practice being on time! Period. What if everyone decided to be "fashionably late?"*
    - *Choose your battles wisely. Pick battles big enough to matter but small enough to win.*

19. What are some of the values you taught your children?
    - *When they were growing up, I always talked with them about life, the value of a good education, loving and being there for each other, and being well-prepared. To this day, I still talk to them this way.*
    - *Continue encouraging them to be the best they can be.*
    - *Be the best parents to their children that they can be.*

20. What do you see as your strengths and positive traits?
    *Resilient, Overcomer, Hard-Working, Family Man, Goal-Oriented, Loving Spirit, Giving Heart, Positive Attitude, Integrity, Honest, Mature, Self-Confident, Protective.*

# My Journey

*I always tried to hold our family together (brothers and sisters) and be there when someone in the family needed me. For this reason, I've always considered myself the "link" in our family, no pun intended. This has nothing to do with my name. It has to do with the fact that I grew up with Bobby, Acy, and Larry, and yet I always stayed in close contact with my younger siblings so I could have a relationship with them. So, I have felt like a "bridge" connecting the two groups of siblings so we could remain a close-knit family. Because, as I always say, "We're all we got!"*

21. What are some of the things you enjoy doing in your leisure time?

    *As I have gotten older, I enjoy watching TV (mostly news, UFO Documentaries, and an occasional movie) much more than I did when I was younger. I love playing golf, and I also love traveling, especially to tropical islands. I love being close to the water.*

22. What are some of your talents/unique traits?

    *My unique traits include being an effective and dedicated leader. (a coach at one of my schools described me as a "Natural" My father was a leader and my brother, Acy, said he believes that is where I got my leadership skills.)*
    *Compassionate and Supportive; Provides Encouragement and Guidance to Others, Giving Spirit, Love of Family. (I think I inherited these traits from my mother.)*

# My Journey

## Chapter XV: Summary – Three Phases of Our Life Together

Early on in our marriage, I shared with Snow my thoughts on how I envisioned our life together. I shared the following:

**FIRST PHASE OF OUR LIFE**

I shared with Snow the first part of our life should focus on finishing college and establishing ourselves in our careers. After finishing college, I talked about the need for us to *"find **our place** in this world."* We had to decide where we would eventually settle down and establish our home because we moved around a lot during the first few years. I honestly feel like I had legitimate reasons for all the moving that I put my family through.

# My Journey

When we started in Brinkley, Arkansas, I never intended to remain there because my entire family had already moved away. I stayed the first year out of college because while completing my "Student Teaching," I was given a contract to return and teach in that position the following year. I saw this as an advantage because after my graduation, I would not have to go looking for a job, as most college graduates did. So, I stayed in Brinkley for my first full year of teaching.

During that year, however, I made up my mind we would move to Flint, Michigan, at the end of the school term. Primarily because the salary was meager, and I missed being around my family. My mom and younger siblings had moved to St. Louis, Missouri. My father and his "new family" had moved to Chicago, Illinois, and my older brothers lived in Flint, Michigan.

After two years in Flint, Snow and I were both ready to leave for various reasons, so we moved to Bronx, New York, where her family lived. After teaching in New York for a few years, I got laid off from my teaching position. At that point, we decided Dallas, Texas, was a good choice to explore because my graduate school professors had talked about Dallas needing teachers. Also, it didn't hurt that Snow had two brothers already living in Dallas. Ultimately, I just wanted to find the *"right place"* for my family while my sons were still very young, and Dallas turned out to be that place.

**SECOND PHASE OF OUR LIFE**

This would be the time we would devote to properly raising our children and providing for their needs. This included encouraging them to work hard in school, graduate from college, and become established in their careers. During this phase, I shared with Snow we would have to make some tough choices and sacrifice many of the things we wanted to ensure our sons had what they needed. I told her *our time* would come.

I must pause here and give credit to my beautiful wife because she was always willing to do what was best for our children. We didn't give them everything they **wanted**, but we certainly tried to give them the things they **needed**! So much so they would ask us if we were rich. We would tell them no and ask them why they thought so. They said their friends always asked them if we were rich because we always tried to ensure our children had what they needed.

NOTE: Dallas turned out to be the "right fit" for my family and me, and I have been very pleased with this choice because Dallas has served us well! Snow enjoyed a career with Delta Airlines, and I had a very successful career working in education. All three of my sons graduated from college and are gainfully employed.

# My Journey

**THIRD PHASE OF OUR LIFE**

IT'S OUR TIME! I told Snow that if we manage Phases One and Two right, Phase Three would be a time for us to live life to the fullest and go and do whatever our hearts desired.

I think we did a pretty good job in Phases One and Two, and we can now enjoy Phase Three – IT'S OUR TIME! Even though we moved around a lot when we were young, we finally settled in Dallas, where we established our careers and provided for our children. We also love and are very proud of our seven wonderful grandchildren.

We have also been able to travel and visit many places, such as The Bahamas (twice), Cancun, and Aruba. We have taken a cruise to Cozumel and Progresso, Mexico. In the U.S., we have visited some of the major cities such as Washington D.C., Baltimore, Philadelphia, New York City, Atlanta, Miami, Orlando, Tampa, Birmingham, Montgomery, Memphis, Detroit, Chicago, St. Louis, New Orleans, Oklahoma City, Tulsa, Houston, Galveston, Albuquerque, Denver, Phoenix, Las Vegas, Los Angeles, Seattle, Myrtle Beach, and many more. We have also enjoyed vacationing in Hawaii on two occasions. We have been truly blessed!

# APPENDICES

## Appendix A:

Quotes that have helped guide my thoughts and actions through the years.

*"Tough Times Never Last, But Tough People Do!"* Dr. Robert Schuller

*"Where one begins does not have to determine where one ends up. Your origins and background do not limit your potential."* Dr. Israel Tribble

*"Education is our passport to the future; for tomorrow belongs only to those who prepare for it today."* Malcolm X

*"Never let someone else's opinion of you become your reality."* Les Brown

*"You cannot go back and change the beginning, but you can start where you are and change the ending."* C. S. Lewis

*"What you DO speaks so loud that I cannot hear what you SAY!"* Ralph Waldo Emerson

*"It is better to be prepared and not wanted than to be wanted and not prepared."* Whitney M. Young

*"I can do all things through Christ who strengthens me."* Phil. 4:13

*"To whom much is given, much will be required."* Luke 12:48

# My Journey

## Appendix B:

Excerpts from Letters and Cards from Relatives, Parents, Teachers, and Administrators I received over the years.

### Messages From Family Members

Card and Note from Acy Butler *(Brother)*
Sometimes the ones who work THE HARDEST and give THE MOST are the quietest about what they've done. That's called HONOR. They INSPIRE the rest of us. That's called PRIDE. Thanks for all you are and all you do.

*"Linc, you're quite a man. May the Lord always bless you."*
**Love, Acy**

Note From Brenda Morrison *(Sister)*
*"Linc, we tend to not tell our loved ones how we feel about them until oftentimes it's too late. So, I want to let you know right here and now that I love you. I am so appreciative of the accomplishments you have made in society and within our family, especially how you have helped mama financially. I know it was not always easy, but you've never complained about doing*

# My Journey

*anything for your family. You've always been there with a willing hand and a smiling face. Thank you for being a loving husband, father, and brother. Thank you for being you. I love you."*

**Brenda**


Note From Gary Pighee *(Nephew)*

*"Uncle Linc, you've been the ideal uncle and role model throughout the years. You've been there throughout my life lending support. I even remember the Honor Roll deal and how you would give me money as an incentive. I was happy to see you there in my hour. I've often looked upon you as a cornerstone in the family. You've been there when people needed you. Your nephew truly appreciated it. Thanks for keeping it real."*

**Your nephew, Gary**


Note From Michael Butler *(Son)*

*"Dad, I am proud to be your son. You have been there for me through thick and thin. You left New York en route to Texas to provide a better life for your wife and sons. Definition of a real man."*

**Love always, Mike**

**Messages From Teachers and Administrators**

# My Journey

Note From Chandra Cooper, Former Teacher @ A. S. Johnston

*"Mr. Butler, I wanted to take a minute to thank you. I also wanted to assure you I could not have asked for a better first-time experience. While I am excited about my new experience, it's important that you know I am leaving Johnston with a saddened heart. (It's always difficult to leave home.) I hope we will continue to keep in contact. Thanks again for what you have done for me and all the experiences you have provided."*

**Chandra Cooper**

Note From Margaret Hazen, Former Teacher @ A. S. Johnston

*"Mr. Butler, thank you for making this another great year to be a teacher. You're wonderful to work for. We're sure glad you're ours."*

**M. Hazen**

Message From Melissa Lawson, Assistant Principal, A. S. Johnston

*"Dear Mr. Butler, I want to thank you for the entire past year of working together. You have certainly given me a high level of achievement to aim for. I continue to be in awe of all of your*

# My Journey

accomplishments at Johnston, and the way you mold and shape the staff to meet our goals. Thank you for the opportunity to work alongside of you and learn from the best!"

**Ms. Lawson**


Message From Penny Coney, Assistant Principal, A. S. Johnston

"Dear Lincoln, thank you for a wonderful experience at Albert Sidney Johnston. Although my stay was brief, I cannot begin to tell you how much I learned from you, and not just the 'principal stuff.' Your leadership style, your integrity and your unflagging optimism inspired not only me, but also your staff and students. I will say with pride that I was a Johnston Falcon!"

**Fondly, Penny**


Messages From the **Parents** of Two of My Teachers


Letter From Dr. Carolyn Cooper, Mother of Chandra Cooper- Former Johnston Teacher

"Dear Mr. Butler, I know it is not often you receive a letter from a parent of one of your former teachers, but I felt the need to write and express my appreciation for your guidance and concern for my daughter, Chandra. When she arrived at Johnston six years

# My Journey

*ago as a brand-new teacher, she was eager and ready to learn. Under your guidance, she has evolved into a self-assured and confident person who will be able to make her way in the field of education wherever she may go. You certainly gave her many opportunities that enhanced her teaching abilities and educational experiences. In addition, your fatherly nurturance was most appreciative by her grandparents and me as we are so many miles away from her. We all send our grateful thanks to you. Best wishes for a successful and rewarding school year."*

**Sincerely, Carolyn I. Cooper**

Message From Ms. Patricia Washington, Mother of one of my Johnston Teachers

*"Mr. Butler, words cannot adequately describe how grateful I am for your consideration and assistance in providing my daughter, Kimetra 'Kim' with her first teaching job. I appreciate you and the vote of confidence you have for her. Please, please let me know if I can ever be of assistance to you or the school. Thanks again!!"*

**Pat Washington**

# My Journey

## Appendix C:

Special Recognitions/Awards

Throughout my professional career, I received numerous awards and recognition for my work. Below is a listing of some of the major awards:

- "Teacher of the Year" at Bushman Elementary – 1981
- "LINCOLN BUTLER APPRECIATION DAY" – Bushman Elementary – 1986
- Dads' Club Outstanding Volunteer Group Service by Dallas County Volunteer Association – 1990
- "Citizen of the Year Award" from Omega Psi Phi – 1996
- "Outstanding Elementary Educator of the Year" by the Oak Cliff Chamber of Commerce – 1998
- State Representative Helen Giddings recognized principal for School Improvement Performance – 2000
- The Seattle Public School District selected principal to Conduct Workshops for Administrators at the Principals Leadership Institute – 2001 (Seattle, Washington)
- "Principal of the Year Award" for Area 5 – 2001
- African American Educators' Hall of Fame Induction – April 2012

# My Journey

## AAEAHP

## 2012 HALL OF FAME INDUCTEE
## MR. LINCOLN BUTLER, SR.

He began his career as a high school social studies teacher at the school from which he had graduated in Brinkley, AR. From there, he worked for the boards of education in Flint, MI, Bronx, NY, and finally, Dallas, TX as a teacher and coordinator of special programs. After serving one year as assistant principal at B. F. Darrell, he was promoted to principal of W. W. Bushman. Additionally, he served as principal of T. W. Browne M. S., Adelle Turner, A. S. Johnston, and Cedar Hill H. S. While principal at Johnston, the school was recognized by the Dallas Foundation and DISD (1996-2002) for School Improvement Performance. Butler's Reading Well was named in his honor at A. S. Johnston.

*The above photo and short bio are displayed in the African American Museum in Dallas, Texas.*

# My Journey

## African American Education Archives and History Program
## Hall of Fame Induction Ceremony - Class of 2012

I was very pleased and honored that my wife, children, brothers and sisters, family members, special friends, Omega Brothers, and colleagues attended this ceremony and supported me. My sincere thanks to each of you!

# My Journey

THE BUTLER FAMILY

Lincoln & Dorothy

# My Journey

Lincoln & Fraternity Brother Bernard Snowden

Thurman Gilbert *(My Brother)* & Lincoln Butler

# My Journey

## Poem

### "See It Through" by Edgar A. Guest

The Poem helped get me through some tough times in my life! I recommend reading it for encouragement when needed!

## Songs

### "We're Gonna Make It" by Little Milton

When we were struggling financially, Snow and I often listened to this song. We would say to each other that we were going to make it: NO MATTER WHAT! We were determined that we were NOT going to give up.

### "Inseparable" by Natalie Cole

When Snow and I wanted to express our deep love for each other, this was our *Go to Song*

### "You're The One" by Hallerin Hill and Lisa Shipman

Snow and I love this song and we danced to it when we renewed our Wedding Vows on July 11, 2011.

My Journey

# Lincoln & Dorothy Snow Butler

**It's so wonderful to know you'll always be around.**

# My Journey

## Words of Encouragement

**REMEMBER:**

**HARD WORK AND PERSISTENCE *WILL* PAY OFF.**

**THE BOTTOM LINE:**

*You do what you have to do to achieve your goals in life. Often, this will mean making many personal sacrifices along the way to reach your destiny!*

LOVE TO ALL OF YOU,

# Lincoln Butler Sr.

(Husband, Father, Grandfather, Brother, Uncle, Cousin, Friend, & Colleague)

Made in the USA
Columbia, SC
28 January 2023